CHANGE YOUR LIFE IN AN HOUR

FOR PETER, MY ROCK –
AND IMMY, MY STAR!

Hardie Grant

QUADRILLE

LAURA ARCHER

CHANGE YOUR LIFE IN AN HOUR

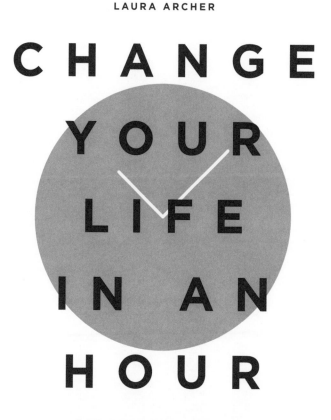

DON'T BELIEVE YOU CAN?
YOU'RE ALREADY DOING IT...

CONTENTS

HEAD

ENGAGE WITH YOUR MIND

MEDITATION 20

YOGA 26

THERAPY 29

WRITING 34

PUZZLES 38

ENGAGE WITH OTHER MINDS

READ 40

LOOK AT ART 43

DEBATE 46

LISTEN 50

GO TO A LIVE PERFORMANCE 54

HEART

CONNECTIONS

LOVE YOURSELF 64

NOURISH
YOURSELF 70

ENHANCE YOUR
CONNECTIONS 76

PORTRAITS 81

LOVE LETTERS 84

VIBRATIONS

SING 86

DANCE 88

LAUGH 91

LISTEN TO YOUR
FAVOURITE TUNES 94

ENJOY NATURE 96

HANDS

TIDY

MAKE BASKETS 104

MAKE MUSIC 108

SEW 112

KNIT (OR CROCHET)
118

MACRAMÉ 122

MESSY

PRINT 126

GARDEN 130

WORK WITH CLAY 134

BAKE 138

EXERCISE 140

Every day, we are all making life-changing decisions.

How we choose to spend our time – whether it's hanging out with friends and family, working, relaxing, or absentmindedly scrolling through social media – has a direct impact on the rest of our day, week, month... and potentially even our life. Our mental health, emotional wellbeing and physical status are re-routed (or rather not) every day, depending on the stimulus we choose to surround ourselves with. So, even if you think you're not, every day you are changing your life.

Unfortunately, we often do exactly the same things day-in, day-out, spending most of those theoretically life-changing moments on auto-pilot, feeling like we're in Groundhog Day and *waiting* for someone or something to pull us out. I used to spend hours

dreaming of escaping my life and being carried away to a new, better version of myself. One that had more energy, less resentment, more interesting anecdotes, and who wasn't, again, *waiting* for something to 'happen' to them. After a while it started to dawn on me that whoever or whatever I was waiting for wasn't coming to get me so, one day, I decided to stop waiting.

"SOMETHING'S GOT TO CHANGE"

I remember the moment I made the decision. It was the grimmest of grim, January days. Quite literally everything was grey: the sky, the pavement, the concrete walls of my office. I was running along a high-walk in central London, having just bought my lunch from the shop across the road, while the rain and wind did their best to push me off course. I had just started a new job, which wasn't turning out to be what I'd expected, the relationship I was in was fragile and confusing, and ultimately life seemed to be going in the opposite direction to where I wanted to be. As I pitched myself diagonally into the wind, clutching my coat and a soggy sandwich, I remember thinking, "Something's got to change".

If I had had energy, nerve, and a healthy savings account, maybe I would have chucked in the job and the boyfriend, gone travelling and found myself – à la *Eat, Pray, Love*. But sadly I didn't, so instead of thinking about what I could cut out of my life, I thought about what I could add in. What was I lacking?

I realized that what upset me most was that I was losing time to things I didn't care so much about and not spending it on the projects, people and dreams that were important to me. I decided I was going to start giving these things time. Evenings and weekends were busy, but I realized I wasn't taking my lunch breaks, usually eating and working at my desk throughout. Suddenly I had found five hours a week purely for myself. I started to use them and was shocked by what I discovered: it turned out that I didn't have to throw my whole life out of the window in order to change it. The things I did with my 20–60 minute lunch breaks brought just as much colour, fascination, relief and opportunity to my life as a total re-start would have done.

"When we are no longer able to change a situation, we are challenged to change ourselves."
— VIKTOR FRANKL

CHANGE YOUR LIFE IN AN HOUR

This book is a development of everything I've learned since that grey day and soggy sandwich. The most obvious revelation is that we don't have to limit ourselves to lunch breaks: we can focus on changing our lives any time of the day: any small chunk of time will do. And despite the book's title, it doesn't have to be a full hour. If you only have 20 minutes, that's fine too.

The next big learning has been how much my whole body is invested in this life-changing process. Along with wanting to bring more colour and intrigue into my life, the decision to start using my lunch breaks for myself was also part-experiment to see if certain activities would help me be more productive at work in the afternoons: it was about concentration and brain power. What I found instead was that, alongside my brain, other parts of me started buzzing too. My hands felt stretched and powerful after I spent time hand-writing, drawing, or knitting. My heart swelled when I sang, meditated, or even when I just sat in a park and looked at a beautiful view. Suddenly these parts of me that I had neglected started to make themselves known. This wasn't just mental activity, but also emotional and physical.

It's for this reason that the book is structured around the head, heart and hands. It's asking you to think about your health and activity in these areas. Do you want to optimize your mental health? Is your heart feeling neglected? Is your body twitching? Think about which part of your life you want to start changing. Naturally, the rest will follow.

THIS IS NOT
A LIFE-HACK

It's important to say that this book is not a life-hack. You won't do one thing for one hour and suddenly your whole life has changed. This book is about habits, about changing your own a small amount each day and, over time, changing your life as a result: for example, in the way you engage with people or ideas, or your sense of peace and fulfilment.

To give this idea context, think about our attitude towards physical fitness and health. If we think our arms are flabby, we might do exercises specifically for toning them; or if our cholesterol is high, we cut down on saturated fats. Sadly, we don't tone up or improve our health after just one session at the gym, or one healthy meal: we need to put in consistent, regular effort to see results over time.

This book is full of 'exercises' and 'diet tips' for our mental, emotional and physical health, so that when you come home from a stressful meeting, or if you're suffering from heartbreak, you have a few things to try that will offset the load. Not all of them will appeal, in the same way that some people love circuit training while other people prefer rock-climbing, so in no way should you see this as a checklist of activities you have to get through. Instead, think of it like a recipe book – when you decide you want to give something a go, you have the full list of ingredients and the method at your fingertips. This is the basis of the whole philosophy of this book and it applies to all sections: head, heart and hands.

"As a single footstep will not make a path on the earth, so a single thought will not make a pathway in the mind. To make a deep physical path, we walk again and again. To make a deep mental path, we must think over and over the kind of thoughts we wish to dominate our lives."
— HENRY DAVID THOREAU

DON'T BLAME YOUR PHONE!

The other thing to mention is that this book isn't about denying yourself the things you love. Like I said, it's not so much about cutting things out as it is about adding things in, or rather improving the amount of time and quality you invest in the good things. Phones and social media often take the blame for a lot of our own inability to spend time positively but, as a wise friend once told me, the first thing you've got to do in any co-dependent relationship is acknowledge the part you've played in getting into it. Our phones distract us because we let them — just as a lover or friend who calls us incessantly does so because, at the start of the relationship, part of us enjoyed the attention and allowed them to establish this pattern of behaviour. It's ok to spend your life-changing 'hour' on the internet, as long as whatever you're reading, watching or scrolling through online brings growth and positivity — whether this is a video tutorial, your favourite film director's life works, or even a generous and informative Instagram account.

RECLAIM AND REPURPOSE

Effectively, this whole book is about 'positive browsing', both online and offline. This might be a familiar idea when it comes to technology (we

all know that we should
turn our notifications
off, set intentions for
why we are going online
and stick to them, limit
screen time etc.), but how
many of us apply this
philosophy to our offline
life? The following pages
will hopefully make you
think about what – or
even who – your *physical*
distractions and time-
drains are, and help you
reclaim and repurpose time
spent negatively with more
positive, creative and life-
enhancing intentions.

"Very little is needed to
make a happy life; it is all
within yourself, in your
way of thinking."
— MARCUS AURELIUS

ENGAGE WITH YOUR MIND	ENGAGE WITH OTHER MINDS
MEDITATION	READ
YOGA	LOOK AT ART
THERAPY	DEBATE
WRITING	LISTEN
PUZZLES	GO TO A LIVE PERFORMANCE

HEAD

First mind-blowing fact: the brain consists of about one trillion cells with 100 trillion connections between those cells. Try to visualize that volume – all inside your head.

Second mind-blowing fact: though it's hard to say, at a rough estimate, scientists suggest the brain is handling 10 quadrillion instructions per second. This puts our normal perception of multi-tasking into perspective, and also explains why we still know so little about the brain and how it functions: there is just so much going on in there, every second of the day.

What we do know, though, is that our brains (and minds) deal with pretty much everything, so we need to look after them. Luckily, we're in a fortunate place in our history for doing this. In the last few years, awareness around the importance of good mental health has risen to a point where most people are comfortable talking about it as part of daily conversation. In fact, one of the more positive consequences of the Covid-19 lockdown was that it made us check in with our friends and family and ask about their mental health on a regular basis. The communal crisis made us unafraid to admit that managing our mental health is a daily undertaking.

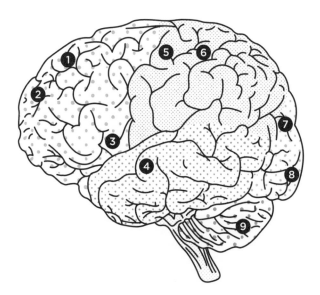

FRONTAL LOBE

1. Eye and head movements
2. Behaviour and emotion
3. Speech

TEMPORAL LOBE

4. Hearing

PARIETAL LOBE

5. Basic movements
6. Sensation

OCCIPITAL LOBE

7. Visual recognition
8. Vision

CEREBELLUM

9. Balance and muscle coordination

OUR MINDS NEED WORKOUTS

We all have mental health, because we all have minds; just as we all have physical health, because we all have bodies. As our bodies go through good phases and bad phases based on internal and external factors, so do our minds. And just as we can help our bodies through things like diet and exercise, it's also possible to work on supporting and benefiting our minds based on what we input to them.

The aim of this section of the book is to get to know how your mind works, so that on days when those anxiety-inducing thoughts that go around and around in your head pop up, you'll know how to move away from them; or on days when you need a bit of fresh stimulus, you'll have a few places to seek it from.

Effectively this is mindfulness. I used to think that mindfulness was contemplating nature or meditating. It's true that these activities are *part* of mindfulness, but the actual act of mindfulness is gaining an awareness of how your mind works, so that you know when it might be *useful* to contemplate nature or meditate. It might also include knowing when it's useful to call a friend or paint a picture. For this reason, there are two parts to this section: engaging with your mind (self-awareness), and engaging with other minds (expanding your thinking).

INSIDE YOUR HEAD

When you have a thought, an electrical signal passes back and forth between the various neurons responsible for that thought. The brain is always trying to become more efficient, so every time two cells communicate, the brain builds a connection that makes it easier for them to do so in the future.

While this is good, because it develops our knowledge network and our ability to react or respond to something quickly, at times this can also have its downside. When we think or experience the same thought over and over again, the connection that has been formed between certain cells becomes more established and therefore more prevalent. Think of it like a shortcut worn into the grass by numerous walkers, who decided not to stick to the longer pathway. Unless you make a conscious decision to stick to the pathway, you will always take the shortcut, because it will get you to your destination more quickly. This can result in rigid thinking: when you have told yourself (or been told) something for so long that a thought pattern becomes so firmly established you find it hard to think or see things in any other direction. Unfortunately, this is particularly harmful if the thought is a negative one.

Luckily, research has shown that throughout life the connections between neurons are continuously growing and changing. This is referred to as neuroplasticity: 'neuro' from neuron, and 'plasticity' meaning the ability of something to change or be moulded. When you practise learning or thinking in new ways, you create new pathways. This is an option that we have throughout our lives: no matter how old you are or what your situation is, you can change the structure of your brain and improve the way you think — it just takes practice! The first part of this section is therefore dedicated to getting to know your own thought patterns, so that you can understand how to control and change them.

OUTSIDE YOUR HEAD

Every thought we have is based on something we have learnt from an external source. This might be a physical event, a person very close to us – such as a parent, sibling or friend – or something far, far away, such as a movie, book or a religious teaching. In the latter case, it might be separated from us by centuries or even millennia. Our learning can be both conscious and subconscious; directly downloaded, or assimilated over time. However we came to know or believe something, it got into our minds through sensory experience. In other words, everything internal has an external beginning.

The more of this external stimulus you put into your brain, the broader our understanding of the world and our place within it becomes. It makes us more confident, more sociable and more creative. Artists are typically encouraged to expand their experience of the world as much as they can, so that their work becomes more complex and fascinating. Our minds are just the same: we need to keep feeding them in order to keep them healthy and growing. The second part of this section looks at engaging with other minds, so that you can expand your way of thinking and avoid becoming too introspective.

A BIT ABOUT MENTAL HEALTH CONDITIONS

This isn't a psychology book and I certainly don't want to give the impression that I believe we can just 'think' away chronic depression, anxiety or trauma. These conditions are devastating for those living with them and often do need additional professional help. Understanding the root of the thought or feeling is always the first step to healing and renewal, and if you are in a situation where you are able to seek help with coming to understand your thought processes and mental health, it will always be a benefit. If it feels like the suggestions included in the following pages only skim the surface, a section on seeking a therapist is included on page 29.

MEDITATION

If you want to engage with your own thoughts, you need to let them be heard first.

Our days are often so packed with other people's thoughts – coworkers, friends, children, partners, journalists, politicians – that we have very little time to give our own mind the space it needs to download what we are thinking and sort things out. Then suddenly we find ourselves awake in the middle of the night, minds racing as we chew over a problem that just won't let us return to sleep until we have given it a proper amount of air time.

Meditation provides a fantastic space for this to happen. By focusing intently on a single thing – whether it is a sound, a sensation or a mantra – all those external voices fall away and we are left to observe our own thoughts. Meditation often brings clarity and a sense of perspective to our worries, as our minds slow and we gain the distance needed to observe things calmly. As a result, meditation has been shown to lower blood pressure, help to reduce anxiety, ease symptoms of depression and improve sleep.

There are lots of different types of meditation, with some suiting certain minds better than others. If you've tried meditation before, but found it more stressful than calming, there's a chance you just haven't found the right one yet. Have a browse through some of the most popular types below and see what sounds most appealing to you. Even if you don't meditate intentionally, you will probably find that you are already practising aspects of particular forms of meditation, which gives you a good place to start.

TYPES OF MEDITATION

MINDFULNESS MEDITATION.

GOOD FOR: Concentration and awareness; easily practised alone.

GENERAL IDEA: Mindfulness encourages you to pay attention to your thoughts as they pass through your mind. You don't judge or become involved with them. You simply observe and take note of any patterns.

HOW TO DO IT: Sitting comfortably in a peaceful location, close your eyes; breathe in through your nose and out through your mouth. Concentrate on the sensation of your breath on each inhale and exhale. This should allow you to observe any bodily sensations, thoughts or feelings. Notice any patterns – do you loop round in anxious circles, or do you always assume defeat before you've tried something? Any time you find your mind wandering, bring your concentration back to your breath.

MANTRA MEDITATION.

GOOD FOR: People who don't like silence and enjoy repetition.

GENERAL IDEA: Mantra meditation uses a repetitive sound to clear the mind. It can be a word, phrase or sound, such as the popular 'Om'. After chanting the mantra for some time, you will be more alert and in tune with your environment. This allows you to experience deeper levels of awareness.

HOW TO DO IT: Find a sound that is calming and that you have uncomplicated associations with. In a peaceful place, make yourself comfortable, close your eyes and focus on the sound. If the mantra is not a sound you are making yourself, make sure that there is a way it can be continuous and uninterrupted (e.g. playing it on repeat if you are using a recorded sound).

TRANSCENDENTAL MEDITATION.

GOOD FOR: Those who like structure and are serious about maintaining a meditation practice.

GENERAL IDEA: Similar to mantra meditation, but more easily customized. Most guided meditation classes follow Transcendental Meditation, using a mantra or series of words that are specific to each practitioner.

HOW TO DO IT: Find a meditation leader – either at a class or through an online session or app – whose practice you can relate to. You might need to try a few different classes before you find the right

one. Once you have, just turn up, make yourself comfortable, and follow their visualizations.

SPIRITUAL MEDITATION.

GOOD FOR: Those who thrive in silence and seek spiritual growth.

GENERAL IDEA: Spiritual meditation is practised in many religions. It's similar to prayer in that you reflect on the silence around you and seek a deeper connection with your God or Universe. It is often a good way of putting your thoughts into perspective.

HOW TO DO IT: Spiritual meditation can be practised at home or in a place of worship. If it is part of your religion, then you will likely have established rituals. It is typical to focus on an object of devotion and to contemplate one's own humility in the face of magnificence. Essential oils and incense are often used to lift the experience away from the corporal.

FOCUSED MEDITATION.

GOOD FOR: Anyone who requires additional focus in their life.

GENERAL IDEA: Focused meditation involves concentration using any of the five senses. For example, you can focus on something internal like your breath, or you can bring in external influences to help focus your attention. Try counting mala beads, listening to a gong or staring at a candle flame.

HOW TO DO IT: Unlike mindfulness where you observe your thoughts, the aim of focused meditation is to try and quieten your thoughts altogether, so that you are purely in the present moment. This practice may be simple in theory, but it can be difficult for beginners to hold their focus for longer than a few minutes at first. If your mind does wander, simply refocus and begin again. It will become easier with regular practice.

MOVEMENT MEDITATION.

GOOD FOR: People who find peace in action and prefer to let their minds wander.

GENERAL IDEA: Movement meditation can include any form of gentle action that allows your mind to wander, whether it's yoga, walking through the woods, gardening, qigong or other gentle forms of motion.

HOW TO DO IT: Choose a form of movement that you know well, so that the action doesn't require your attention. Walking is a popular choice. Eighteenth-century French philosopher Jean-Jacques Rousseau famously stated, "I can only meditate when I am walking. When I stop, I cease to think; my mind only works with my legs."

A FEW THINGS TO CONSIDER BEFORE YOU BEGIN

HOW YOU ARE.

The frame of mind you are in when you come to the meditation is important. Even if you are only going to meditate for 20 minutes, think about the 10 minutes leading up to and away from this time. Work out how to create a buffer around your meditation time so that you can prepare and reflect – put a movie on for the kids, put your phone on airplane mode, meditate just after a shower when you are feeling refreshed and focused. The time on either side of your meditation is the bridge from the external to the internal world – if the bridge isn't there, you'll struggle to reach the destination.

WHERE YOU ARE.

The physical space you are in is also important. Find somewhere warm and soothing, a place where that you feel safe enough to close your eyes and shut off from the outside world. If you're meditating while commuting, choose a corner seat where no one will disturb you by trying to step over you; wear good headphones so you can block out the sounds around you. If you're at home or in a meditation space, think about dimming the lights, lighting candles or scenting the room with essential oils (either heating them in a diffuser or putting some on a tissue and inhaling) or by burning incense or smudge sticks.

HERBS AND OILS TO BRING THE ZEN HOME:

Frankincense, myrrh, sage, cedar, sandalwood, palo santo.

GUIDED OR UNGUIDED?

The two main ways to meditate are guided and unguided. If you've never meditated before, try a couple of guided meditations first – either in person at a meditation class or online via a video tutorial or app – as they will give you an understanding of how to get into the meditation, as well as how to refocus when your mind wanders, and how to come out of the meditation calmly. Once you have this structure, you might find that you prefer silence or just background music.

A WORD ABOUT APPS.

There are lots of apps that will help you with guided meditation, though the two frontrunners are Calm and Headspace. Both can be trialled for free, after which you pay a subscription. Both apps will ask you to choose your area of focus at the start (better sleep, work and productivity, etc.) and will then provide tailored meditations for this, starting with 3–10 minutes a day. The main differences

are the interfaces, the narrators and the variety of meditations. Give them both a go and see which you prefer.

REMEMBER.

Meditation is something you need to practise – it won't come easily and you might feel like you're no good at first, but keep going and you will be more focused each time. Start small: 5-10 minutes a day is more than enough for beginners.

YOGA

Unlike stretching or fitness, yoga is more than just physical postures.

Yoga is unique because we connect the movement of the body and the fluctuations of the mind to the rhythm of our breath. Connecting the mind, body and breath helps us to direct our attention inward and, similar to meditation, teaches us to recognize our habitual thought patterns without labelling them, judging them or trying to change them. We become more aware of our experiences, and the tensions held in our bodies and minds, from moment to moment.

As with meditation, there are many types of yoga, and both the practice and the teacher will affect your level of engagement and the desired outcome. Don't be shy to shop around a little. Sign up to a membership scheme which provides access to gyms and exercise studios around the country, so that you can try a whole range of classes and venues. If you can't get to a good class easily, have a look through the list of types of yoga below, and find a class on YouTube to practise at home.

Finally, don't let time constraints or unrealistic goals be an obstacle – do what you can and don't worry about it, even if that's only 20 minutes a week. You will likely find that after a while your desire to practise naturally expands and you will find more and more time to devote to it.

TYPES OF YOGA

RESTORATIVE AND YIN YOGA.

GOOD FOR: Total calm and relaxation.

GENERAL IDEA: Possibly the most relaxing way to soothe frayed nerves, restorative and yin yoga classes use bolsters, blankets and blocks to prop students into passive poses so the body can experience the benefits of a pose without having to exert any effort, allowing the mind to fully relax. Studios and gyms often offer these classes on Friday nights, when just about everyone can do with some profound rest.

HATHA.

GOOD FOR: Feeling longer, looser and more relaxed.

GENERAL IDEA: In the West, Hatha yoga has come to be used as a generic term that refers to nearly any type of yoga that teaches physical postures. When a class is marketed as Hatha, it generally means that you will get a gentle introduction to basic yoga postures. You probably won't work up a sweat, but you will still get a good amount of exercise.

VINYASA.

GOOD FOR: People who hate routine and love to test their physical limits.

GENERAL IDEA: Vinyasa is a Sanskrit word for a phrase that roughly translates as 'to place in a special way', referring to a sequence of poses. Vinyasa classes are known for their fluid, movement-intensive practices, sequenced to transition smoothly from pose to pose, with the intention of linking breath to movement. The intensity of the practice is similar to Ashtanga (see below), but no two Vinyasa classes are the same.

ASHTANGA.

GOOD FOR: Working up a sweat.

GENERAL IDEA: Ashtanga is a rigorous style of yoga that follows a specific sequence of postures and is similar to Vinyasa yoga, as each style links every movement to a breath. The difference is that Ashtanga always performs the exact same poses in the exact same order. This is a sweaty, physically demanding practice.

BIKRAM/HOT YOGA.

GOOD FOR: Seriously working up a sweat.

GENERAL IDEA: If ever there was a time not to forget your water bottle, a Bikram or Hot Yoga class is it, as the room temperature is turned up and you sweat like never before while working your way through a series of poses. Though on the surface very similar, the main difference between Bikram and Hot Yoga is the sequence of these poses. Like Ashtanga, a Bikram class always follows the same sequence. This is a wildly popular practice,

making it one of the easiest classes to find.

PRE-NATAL YOGA.

GOOD FOR: Pregnant women, tailored to women in all trimesters.

GENERAL IDEA: Many say that pre-natal yoga is one of the best types of exercise for expectant mums because of the pelvic floor work, focus on breathing and bonding with the growing baby; it also helps mothers prepare for labour and delivery. During this practice you'll use props to modify your poses and ensure stability.

REMEMBER.

Yoga isn't about being the most flexible person in the class. It's about achieving balance between strength and flexibility in your body, which will help achieve balance in your mind. Don't push yourself into uncomfortable poses. Go as far as you feel is right for you, and use bolsters and props to support yourself.

THERAPY

**"There is no greater agony than bearing an untold story inside you."
— Maya Angelou**

Sometimes, no matter how much work we do exploring our own thoughts, we need a bit of help understanding them. Therapy is so beneficial because, no matter how much you think you might have self-analysed or worked your way through a problem, you will always be telling yourself the same story. Remember those neuron connections and prevalent thought patterns mentioned on page 16? Usually, we can only remember our memories one way, because we have 'trodden' that pathway so many times that the brain short circuits to it. A therapist will show you alternative routes. They will pick at little details in your memories – things you

might consider insignificant – and ask you to explore them from a different perspective, thus opening up the problem and, over time, dissipating it.

There isn't a single person who wouldn't benefit from seeing a therapist, but acknowledging that you are one of those people is a big step. There's nothing wrong with needing therapy. In the words of psychologist Dr Nicole LePera (@the. holistic.psychologist), therapists are "not treating mental illness. [They] are treating trauma responses, coping mechanisms, and subconscious programming." Negative thought patterns are usually the result of traumatizing or distressing events and behaviours that have sent our brains into a state of stress, triggering anxiety, depression and a whole other host of monsters. In seeking help from a therapist, you are merely trying to understand how you have subconsciously responded to events or circumstances in the past, so that you gain greater control over your future.

FINDING THE RIGHT THERAPY

Once you have decided that you would like to seek therapy, the next step is understanding the different types of therapy and which is most appropriate for you. A few of the most commonly practised include:

PSYCHODYNAMIC THERAPY helps to resolve emotional conflicts, especially those derived from childhood experience. If you have a recurrent emotional response to a situation or person, but can't understand why,

psychodynamic therapy will help you find and understand the root cause.

PSYCHOANALYTIC THERAPY investigates the interaction of conscious and unconscious elements in the mind, bringing repressed fears and conflicts into the conscious mind by techniques such as dream interpretation and free association.

COGNITIVE THERAPY (also known as cognitive behavioural therapy or CBT) identifies and corrects thought patterns that promote self-defeating attitudes. It's particularly good if you suffer from anxiety or phobias, and normally provides you with a very sturdy, supportive mental structure to help pull you out from this.

BEHAVIOURAL TREATMENT improves social skills and teaches ways to manage stress and unlearn learned helplessness.

INTERPERSONAL THERAPY helps you cope with personal disputes, loss and separation, and transition between social roles.

SUPPORTIVE THERAPY provides advice, reassurance, sympathy and education about the condition. If you are burdened by a long-term mental health illness, this type of therapy will support you day to day.

FINDING THE RIGHT THERAPIST

If you're lucky enough to live in a country where you can seek therapy through a public or national health service, definitely explore your options here. Alternatively, it might be that your employer covers this, either through a workplace service or health insurance. Speak to your HR department and see what the options are.

If you are going private, recommendations are always a great place to start, but don't feel obliged to go with a therapist just because a friend says they are good. This is a huge, life-changing choice you are making – take your time and shop around. Find a therapist who is right for you and your budget.

You can usually search for therapists on the internet, based on your location. This is fantastic but you will get a lot of results, so here are some tips for whittling them down to a shortlist (if this feels like too big a task on top of everything else you're battling with, ask a close friend or relative to help you):

TRUST YOUR GUT.
Most therapists will provide a short description of their practice and approach. Trust your reactions to these descriptions. Does the way they've written make you feel safe and respected, or condescended and

nauseous? Think of it like an online dating profile – do you want more, or are they making you cringe?

GO FOR A COUPLE OF CONSULTATIONS.

If you can't decide between two therapists, book an initial consultation with both of them. Again, think of the dating analogy – it's got to be a true match, so go on a few 'first dates'. This applies for the therapist, too – they normally offer an initial consultation to see if they feel they can offer you the right support. Some therapists offer free consultations, while some charge, so find out before you go booking several, but definitely don't feel afraid to let them know that you're speaking with a few therapists initially, to see who you think would work best with the issues you'd like to address. You don't want to feel locked in with someone that isn't right for you – this is your time after all, not theirs.

BE HONEST ABOUT YOUR EXPECTATIONS.

Do you want a therapist who engages in conversation with you, challenging your statements as you go, or one who just listens, makes notes and feeds back after? Do you want to support your sessions with additional learning – perhaps receiving set reading and homework from your therapist to help you understand your issue on a deeper level – or do you trust that your weekly meeting is enough? Is it important that you feel the therapist is more intelligent than you? Discuss all of this in your initial consultation: ask the therapist what their style of practice is; what their qualifications are; their main areas of focus; why they became therapists. It might feel very direct, but you will be saving both them and you time in the long run.

YOU'RE THROUGH THE DOOR... NOW WHAT?

TRY TO FIND A FOCUS. Some people know the exact issue that they would like to address with a therapist; others have a sense that there is a lot to discuss but don't know where to start. It's absolutely fine if you fall into the second category, but try to use your first couple of sessions to focus in on the issue(s) you would like to explore the most with your therapist. It will give you a sense of progress, and will also empower you to set the pace, especially if you only have the budget for a limited number of sessions.

DON'T LET THE THERAPIST GET PERSONAL. A therapist should never make a judgement or give you their personal opinion. If they do this, especially if it makes you feel self-conscious or ridiculed, it might be time to move on.

REMEMBER YOU'RE IN THE DRIVING SEAT. You are the client, and as such you control what you talk about, and also when you feel you're ready to wrap things up. Be conscious that most therapists will ask for a notice period, so be respectful of this when you are winding things down, but never feel obliged to stay with a therapist for longer than you want to.

REMEMBER.
Therapy looks at thought patterns, beliefs and habits – things that every single person has. By attending therapy, you are merely demonstrating an inquisitive and constructive approach to your own.

WRITING

The physical manifestation of our thoughts into words, through writing, can be one of the most cathartic and revealing exercises.

It provides us with an opportunity for focus, tranquillity, introspection and creativity. Our writing might come to life as a stream of consciousness or as a structured statement; it may have a reader in mind or it might go straight into the waste paper basket – or be hidden in a secret drawer. It's a rare thing that can go in any direction we want it to and an action that stretches across our mental, emotional and physical lives.

Though you can make the focus of your writing anything you want it to be, if you are undertaking this activity with the goal of getting to know your thoughts, make those thoughts the starting point.

This might be:

• One thought in particular that won't go away – a love, a loss, a fear, an anticipation.

• Something you have learned about your way of thinking during meditation.

• A turning point in your life – an event, a conversation, a revelation.

• An attitude or a philosophy that you always carry with you.

Once you have decided what it is that you would like to explore with your writing, think about the format and style of writing that you would like to use. A few ideas include:

JOURNALING.

Chart your thought processes daily or weekly. The purpose of a journal is to get an overview of something over an elongated period of time, so it's best not to overthink what you write in your journal and to use stream of consciousness.

LETTER-WRITING.

Explore your thoughts in a letter to someone you trust – or even to yourself. The benefit of letter-writing is that we are usually conscious of a reader, and therefore take time to construct a well written piece of communication. As such, letter-writing often involves a good deal of reflection, before you commit your thoughts to paper.

STORY-TELLING.

Best suited for recounting memories or events, story-telling is brilliant for making you consider the arc of a narrative, as well as thinking about the perspective you will write it from (maybe not your own?).

POETRY OR LYRIC-WRITING.

When creating a poem or a song, we work to capture the essence of a thought, feeling or happening. This distils emotion into its most potent form and produces a piece of writing that allows us to revisit certain feelings from the past almost in real-time.

REPORTING.

Factual and informative, reporting is a great way to try and explore something without bias, so that you can take a step back and reappraise a situation from an objective point of view.

BEATING WRITER'S BLOCK

You have your subject and your style: now all you need to do is write! However, with writers often revered in most societies, the idea of committing your own thoughts to paper can be daunting. If this is the case, here are a few tips to get you going:

MAKE IT PHYSICALLY ENTICING.

Part of the joy of writing is the feeling of a pen in your hand moving across the paper, so make sure you maximize this pleasure by taking some time to choose your pen and paper carefully. Make them something you look forward to using. If you prefer to type, you could convert this into investing in a new keyboard (if those keys are starting to stick...).

START WITH THE FIRST THING THAT COMES OUT OF YOUR HEAD.

Get all the junk out: the cringe-worthy sentences, the dramatic sentiments, the mundane thoughts. No-one ever needs to read this, not even yourself – it can go straight in the waste basket if you want it to. This is purely a warm-up, to get the juices flowing. Somehow it works and it makes you less scared of carrying on when it comes to the good stuff.

'FIND' SOME WORDS.

This is a fantastic exercise if you're looking at creative writing, poetry or lyric-writing. Take your theme – a memory, a place, a person. Then take a newspaper or magazine and leaf through for some words that grab you, linked to this theme. Limit yourself to ten words to begin with, otherwise it takes a while. Once you have your words, cut them out, arrange them into a statement and stick them down on a piece of paper. You can add in pronouns and conjunctions if needed. You'll be amazed by how stunning and unexpected your compositions are. And yes, they are *your* compositions: you chose the words, and decided how to arrange them on the page. Writing is the same thing, just without the scissors and glue.

SET LIMITATIONS.

Although freedom is essential when writing for yourself, sometimes a lack of structure can be intimidating. If it helps, think about simple limitations like how many words or sides of paper you'd like your writing to take up. Especially in journaling or letter-writing, this can be a good way of making you reflect on what you'd like to say before you start writing, which will help you understand your own thoughts and feelings better.

REMEMBER.

This exercise is for you to explore your thoughts, not to be appointed the next poet laureate. Let yourself go and just see what comes out. In the words of Margaret Atwood, "the waste-paper basket is your friend".

PUZZLES

While puzzles may not strike you as the most obvious hotline to your subconscious, their ability to ground us firmly in the present is actually a fantastic way of allowing us to observe our thoughts – almost a bit like mindfulness.

Depending on the type of puzzle you choose, your mind can either wander, learn to focus more intently, seek distraction from negative or anxious thought patterns, or simply flex its IQ. All the while, in the background, you will also be boosting brain activity and improving your memory – and once you've solved the puzzle or won the game, you'll get that all important hit of dopamine that success always brings with it.

Use the list below to decide which type of puzzle suits your desired outcome and thought process best. Ideally, to reap the benefits, you want something that you can build into a regular routine.

JIGSAW PUZZLES.

Perfect for focused concentration that doesn't require too much intellectual thinking, allowing your mind to wander while your eyes and hands do the work. A good way to bring your heart rate down and therefore calm your thought patterns. Particularly good for anxiety.

BOARD GAMES.

Fantastic for consuming all your thoughts and engaging your problem-solving capabilities. Board games will reveal how you deal with pressure and strategy. They challenge you to think laterally and plan ahead in order to beat your opponent. Some old favourites include chess, Risk, Monopoly, Scrabble, Cluedo, Battleship...

WORD AND NUMBER PUZZLES.

Word and number puzzles are different to board games in that instead of planning ahead, you will scan back through some of your most foundational knowledge and learning. They are also usually collaborative, rather than pitched against an opponent, and so build bridges between your thoughts and another's, leaving you with the satisfaction of well-executed teamwork if you manage to solve the clues.

LOGIC PUZZLES.

A logic puzzle is a problem that can be solved through deductive reasoning. Typical logic puzzles include Sudoku or code-breaking. Logic puzzles are good for training your brain to remain focused and not to give in to distractions, as you have to retain multiple combinations in your mind in order to find the winning arrangement. This type of puzzle is brilliant if you want to shut down repetitive thought patterns and divert your attention to something rational and focused.

REMEMBER.

Although the desire with any puzzle or game is to win, from your mind's point of view, the process is the most important part. If you don't manage to solve it, don't worry that your time and effort have been wasted: they definitely haven't.

READ

While the world around us becomes increasingly driven by stereotypes, generalizations and impulsive big headlines, books offer us a refuge from the noise and an opportunity to engage with another person's thinking in a more intimate, subjective way.

Reading something written by an individual who has devoted months, if not years, to the telling of their story provides us with a more nuanced, considered and expanding narrative. Reading broadens our understanding of the world and our place in it; it develops our empathy, making us more human; it can put things into perspective, soothe, offer solace, rile us up, remind us of our principles or stir us into action!

Though our minds are inundated with words every day – text messages, emails, news feeds – reading for leisure is entirely different because we choose the words. Online, words find us, whether through algorithms or distraction, while offline, they wait for us to pick them up. So, what words and thoughts do you want to pick up? Do you want to expand your understanding of another culture, another gender's experience, or perhaps a certain period in history, or a turning point in attitudes?

CREATE YOUR OWN READING LIST

Do some research and draw up a reading list – start with five books and see how you go. Many journalists and critics have already set out their own reading lists, so you might find some ready-made ones available online. This could be a list that you work your way through over a season, or over several years. The beautiful thing about books is that you can carry them anywhere with you, and their contents will fit into the cracks of your life – during your commute, while moving between meetings, those five minutes of peace you get just before bed. Tailor the list to your own personal development and the broadening of your world.

A few ideas of themes to focus on:
- Works only by non-white or minority writers.
- Works only by female/ male/transgender writers.
- Works set in a particular country.
- Works written around a change in zeitgeist, e.g. female liberation, the machine age, future technologies.

BOOK CLUBS

There's nothing like sharing the joy of a good book, and book clubs are the obvious way to extend this to a circle of friends, coworkers or neighbours. As video call technology has improved, your book club could even extend across borders and continents!

The main challenges with any book club are (1) making sure everyone reads the book in time for the meeting, and (2) getting the conversation into a place that doesn't feel like you're in a Literature class, trying to impress each other with your opinions.

To tackle the first challenge, you could start with works of less than 100 pages, to help everyone get into the rhythm of the book club. The following five classics all fall into this category:

- *The Little Prince* by Antoine de Saint-Exupéry
- *Brokeback Mountain* by Annie Proulx
- *The Old Man and the Sea* by Ernest Hemingway
- *We Should All Be Feminists* by Chimamanda Ngozi Adichie
- *The Strange Library* by Haruki Murakami

To get around the second challenge, try adding a few immersive touches to create a more informal atmosphere. If you're dialling in, all of these can also be done remotely:

- Ask each guest to prepare a dish or bring a drink, linked to the book.
- Set a dress code – again, this could be linked to the book or completely separate.
- Think about how you will light the room (candlelight, bright sunlight, fairy lights etc.).

REMEMBER.

Go for books that intrigue you personally: don't feel obliged to read something just because it's deemed a classic, or it's had a good review. Read for your own growth and enjoyment.

LOOK AT ART

Art can be a tricky encounter.

It's something that so many of us 'love', though when pushed to define why, or what we love, we're often left speechless and embarrassed, and decide we're better off not engaging. Don't do this!

There are so many attempts to define what art 'is', but the most relevant one that I have come across – in relation to engaging with other minds – is that art is that which connects the living and the dead.

This idea works on two levels. First, on an intimate level, art touches us when we get a sense of having shared an experience with the maker, who is usually someone we have never met and is likely separated from us by centuries or continents. It is the sense that an emotion, a view, an encounter, an idea or a sensation that you have experienced personally has been so perfectly described by another person through form, colour, composition or expression, that you know you are not alone in your thoughts and feelings. It crystallizes your experience and connects you to the artist's, cutting through time, nationality, gender and social position. Intellectually, emotionally and spiritually, it connects the living and the dead.

Second, on a broader level, if you consider 'living' and 'dead' to be opposites, good art can also expand your consciousness by making you aware of the 'other'. The 'other' idea, the 'other' experience, the 'other' point of view that you just may have never come into contact with before. It stretches our understanding and puts our own lives into perspective.

Whichever way you look at it, art speaks to us. Here's how to start listening...

KNOW WHAT YOU LIKE

No one wants to get stuck in a conversation with someone (or something) that they have absolutely no interest in. But how do you find that personal connection with an artwork when you've been told that every exhibit in a room is a masterpiece, to be treated with equal reverence? A lot of us enter an exhibition and start with the first work on the left, studiously working our way round every single piece until we're exhausted and just want to head to the café. This is the equivalent of walking into a bar and speaking with every person in there, rather than just going up to the one person who's caught your attention and having a unique, possibly life-enhancing conversation with them.

To discover what you like, you need to be brutal and stop giving time to art that doesn't grab you. The word 'grab' is important here, because this is exactly how it should feel. Discovering an artwork that you like should feel like falling in love, or at least having a crush. You see it across a crowded room and you've just got to go over and find out more.

HOW TO IDENTIFY YOUR ART CRUSH

LET YOUR BODY CHOOSE.

Start with somewhere free. This could be a public gallery or museum, a church or a commercial gallery. Public spaces are better for this exercise because they usually have big collections and therefore more choice. Walk in, and just keep walking fairly quickly past the artworks until your body stops without you consciously intending it to.

Something has caught your attention.

APPROACH.

As soon as you stop, go over to the artwork that has grabbed you and look at it. Try and work out why it made you stop. Was it the colour, the size, the shape, the subject matter? Read the label. If the information provided doesn't answer your questions, google the work or the artist. Once you've read a bit, look at the artwork again. Spend a few minutes just standing in front of it. Immerse yourself fully in the experience – try and make the artwork the only thought in your mind. What can you learn from it? What is it telling you?

GET THE DETAILS.

Finally, before you move on to find your next art crush, take a photo of the artwork and save it in a special folder just for art (make sure you take a photo of the label too so you don't

forget what it is). Do this every time an artwork stops you in your tracks. Over time, you'll build a digital pin board of your art crushes and you'll be able to identify patterns. Do all the works share a theme, a colour, a group of artists or a period in time? Write down what you have learnt from each artwork, or what drew you to it initially. Now when people ask you why or what you love about art, you'll be able to give them a very confident answer.

REMEMBER.
You don't need to like everything.

DEBATE

It's likely you haven't debated since junior school – and even then, unless you were the class star, it was probably terrifying.

But take away the classroom and the fear of being graded (both by your peers and your teacher), and debating is a fantastic way to stretch your mind, engage with other people's stories, experiences and points of view, develop your speaking skills, and enhance confidence in yourself.

It's also brilliant for building your ability to deal with conflict. A debate is a structured *argument*: not in the destructive, 'fighting' sense of the word, but in the constructive, 'presenting a case' sense. In practising debating, you will also be practising how you manage your communication style when emotions and convictions

are running high.

When most of us think of debating, we imagine a very structured event: a panel, a judge, an auditorium with a large audience. If this is what you crave, then a quick online search of local debating societies will give you some good options. But for those of us who are looking to develop our debating skills more privately, these elements don't need to exist. In fact, there doesn't even need to be a winner and a loser. The purpose of this activity, within the context of engaging with other minds, is for you to enjoy the act of researching and learning about your topic, consider something from another person's point of view, and then flex your communication skills by structuring the way you deliver your argument. The debate could take place between you and a best friend, a partner or a family member, perhaps over a meal or a glass of wine, a video call or a walk in the park.

The key here is genuine enjoyment and intrigue. Choose topics that aren't going to damage relationships: although politics and religion always provide a meaty list of topics to unpick, your debate could be about something more light-hearted. You could debate:

- The greatest invention in history
- The best artist/musician/ actor
- The relationship between humans and tech (good/ bad?)
- ...or some small detail that only you and your opponent understand

Again, it's all about really researching your topic, understanding both sides of the argument, and making an objective decision about which side (if either) presents the most compelling case.

Once you've landed on your topic, and decided who is going to argue what, the following tips will help you get the most out of your debate.

THE STRUCTURE OF A GOOD DEBATE

INTRODUCE YOUR ARGUMENT.

Try to summarize in a couple of sentences what your position is and what you will be arguing. The rest of your presentation is for you to explain why you are arguing this. Try to get this done within a maximum of 2 minutes.

EXPLAIN YOUR ARGUMENT CLEARLY.

Structure your case into between two and four

points: no more, no less. Use logic, worked examples, statistics and quotes to support it. This part should take up 4–7 minutes.

HAVE A CONCISE CONCLUSION.

Don't forget to recap the key points again at the end. Try to sum them up in a few bullet points. Make it punchy: again, maximum 2 minutes.

LISTEN AND TAKE NOTES WHEN YOUR OPPONENT IS PRESENTING THEIR ARGUMENT.

Don't interrupt them while they are speaking, save your counter-arguments for the rebuttal (see next point). Above all, don't drift off fantasizing about how intelligent your response is going to be, or you might miss the crux of their argument.

ADDRESS POINTS DIRECTLY IN YOUR REBUTTAL.

Don't use this to voice new arguments of your own that you've just thought of. Respond directly to your opponent's case. Do the facts they've presented ring true? Is their argument morally or logically flawed? Give each other 3–5 minutes for this otherwise you'll forget what the main points are.

AGREE TO AGREE OR DISAGREE.

Unless you have a judge or audience who are voting for one party or the other, find a way to bring the debate to a conclusion. There are two sides to every story (at least). It's fine if this turns out to be your conclusion.

A QUICK WORD ABOUT STYLE

Before you get going, think about how you would like to present your argument. Will you be humorous, emphatic, courteous, assertive? If you're planning a series of debates, try a different style each time and see which helps you get your point across most effectively.

REMEMBER.

Keep it simple. While long words may make you sound clever, they may also make you incomprehensible. Also use notes as a prompt, not a script. There's nothing less conversational than listening to someone read out an essay verbatim.

LISTEN

There's no better way to engage with another person's way of thinking than to actually listen to them talking.

And there's never been a time in history when we've been better placed to do this. From podcasts to radio programmes to TED Talks, we are spoilt for choice when it comes to expanding our worlds by hearing from people and experts from *everywhere* talking about *everything*.

With our options being endless, the very small list below is a starting point from which you can launch yourself into the infinite. It focuses on five of the best podcasts and TED Talks that encourage us to shift our perspective and embrace new ideas:

PODCASTS

HOW TO FAIL WITH ELIZABETH DAY

WHAT? A podcast that celebrates the things that haven't gone right.

HOW LONG? 45–50 minutes

Every week novelist, journalist and broadcaster Elizabeth Day invites a new interviewee to explore what their failures taught them about how to succeed better. A fantastic roster of speakers lends their perspective to this incredibly humbling and uplifting podcast, reminding us that our mistakes are only failures if we don't learn from them...

HEAVYWEIGHT

<u>WHAT?</u> Stories that take you back to the moment everything changed.

<u>HOW LONG?</u> 40–50 minutes

Jonathan Goldstein is not a self-help guru, but that doesn't stop him trying. In every episode, the Heavyweight host takes a guest back to a point in their life where everything changed and helps unravel the mysteries that sprang from that moment. Each episode is as touching as it is funny, as Goldstein bumbles himself and his companion towards some kind of resolution.

ZIGZAG

<u>WHAT?</u> An exploration of the people and companies working to change the world for the better.

<u>HOW LONG?</u> Around 45 minutes

Dubbed 'the business show about being human', host of NPR's TED Radio Hour Manoush Zomorodi profiles a series of unusual dynamos reinventing business, their industries and even capitalism in the name of humanity. Prepare to feel truly fired up about the future.

THE GOOD LIFE PROJECT

<u>WHAT?</u> Inspirational, intimate and disarmingly unfiltered conversations about living a fully engaged, fiercely connected and purpose-drenched life.

<u>HOW LONG?</u> Just over an hour

The Good Life Project began as a personal quest to learn how to live a life of deep meaning, joy and connection. It's now grown into a global community, providing inspirational content and media from 'embodied teachers' – people who don't just talk the talk, but also walk the walk.

THE GURLS TALK PODCAST

WHAT? A safe space to talk about and listen to topics which are considered taboo.

HOW LONG? Around 60 minutes

Growing out of UK model and activist Adwoa Aboah's platform Gurls Talk, guests are invited to share their stories about everything from mental health and dealing with loss, to racial politics and the power of language.

TED TALKS

BRENÉ BROWN

THE POWER OF VULNERABILITY. About the importance of opening yourself up to vulnerability, and dropping the perception that vulnerability is the same as weakness.

SHAWN ACHOR

THE HAPPY SECRET TO BETTER WORK. About shifting your perspective away from one that scans for negativity. A really fun talk to watch, with a lot of laughter.

SUSAN CAIN

THE POWER OF INTROVERTS. About the need for us to culturally shift our perspective from championing extroverts to honouring introverts too.

CHIMAMANDA NGOZI ADICHIE

THE DANGER OF A SINGLE STORY. About the dangers of only considering a single narrative, and the importance of opening your mind up to alternatives.

PAULA STONE WILLIAMS

I'VE LIVED AS A MAN AND A WOMAN – HERE'S WHAT I LEARNED.
About shifting yourself into another person's shoes, while acknowledging the power of your own.

ON YOUTUBE

ALAIN DE BOTTON

WHY YOU WILL MARRY THE WRONG PERSON.
About our misconceptions around love and relationships – including our crazy fairytale expectations – and how we need to be more forgiving and realistic about the fact that our partners will never be perfect, and that's OK!

REMEMBER.
Don't just listen to content that affirms your existing beliefs. Embrace new thinking that will expand your sense of possibility and make your world bigger.

GO TO A LIVE PERFORMANCE

One of the healthiest things for our minds to understand is that we are part of a bigger picture; that there is a multitude of experiences and points of view out there.

Although we can achieve this through reading and listening to stories, there is also a more resonant understanding to be had when watching another human go through an experience. We empathize with their facial expressions, their movements, the tone of their voice. We are in the room with them, sharing an experience in real time.

The energy of a (good) live performance is scintillating. For some reason, you don't get this with a pre-recorded performance, for example the cinema. As fantastic as a movie may be, we're

usually ready for bed when it's over, whereas live performances have us buzzing all the way home. Pre-Covid-19 lockdown, I would have said this was because with a live performance you're in a shared space together and the energy is infectious, but even during lockdown, it's likely that, when you wanted a sense of company, you found yourself gravitating towards live-streams or live-broadcasts more often than pre-recorded ones. There's something about knowing that the person or people who you are watching are right there with you. They have your attention and time, but equally, you have theirs.

SEE MORE STUFF LIVE

What do you already watch or listen to remotely that you could start experiencing live? Begin with what you love, whether it's comedy and sitcoms, movies, podcasts and radio, music... Think about how they could all translate into live performances. Don't push yourself to go along to something completely foreign immediately: of course, you can build up to this as the weeks go by,

but you don't want to scare yourself away by going to something that has you clock-watching and looking for the nearest exit.

Use the table below to think about what you could convert from an 'at home' experience to a live one. Bear in mind how often you'd like to fit this into your life as you will need a budget for this, so be realistic. Lots of small local performances are either free or very low cost, so perhaps start with these as your regular go-to live experience, and treat yourself to a blow-out live performance every so often.

IF YOU LIKE...	THEN SEEK OUT SOME...
Comedy and sitcoms	Live stand-up comedy Theatre, particularly farce
Epic movies, high drama, big emotions	Opera, ballet, theatre (immersive theatre or immersive cinema is especially good for this)
Podcasts, radio, TED Talks	Live podcast and broadcast recordings, lectures, talks, panel discussions
Music, lyrics, poetry, spoken word	Gigs, concerts, musicals, spoken word events
Mind-blowing physical feats	Circus, ballet, contemporary dance

BE CRITICAL

Make sure you research something before you go and see it. Read reviews: be critical of the storyline, or the interpretation of it. Does it sound like something you want to sit or stand through? There's an assumption that live performances – especially if they are the work of a national theatre, opera, ballet or orchestra – are innately good and that we will have a transformative experience when we go to see them. But this can sometimes be far from the truth. Although you're part of an audience, your experience of the performance is a personal one. Be realistic about where you want to put yourself.

REMEMBER.

We've all had a bad experience with a live performance, but don't let that put you off – we've also all seen bad movies or TV shows, but that didn't mean we stopped watching TV altogether. If you went to the theatre once and swore you'd never go again, give a different venue a go.

CONNECTIONS

LOVE YOURSELF

NOURISH YOURSELF

ENHANCE YOUR
CONNECTIONS

PORTRAITS

LOVE LETTERS

VIBRATIONS

SING

DANCE

LAUGH

LISTEN TO YOUR
FAVOURITE TUNES

ENJOY NATURE

HEART

As a society that teaches empiricism (the theory that all knowledge comes primarily from sensory experience), our hearts sometimes get left behind, as we are encouraged to listen to our heads first.

But a growing amount of research is showing just how important it is to be engaged with our passions and emotions – not only for emotional and mental wellbeing, but also for physical health.

THE EMOTIONAL HEART

Though it's proven that emotions are created in the brain, it is equally acknowledged that they are felt, or physically experienced, in the heart. When we hear bad news, we often say we 'feel our heart drop'; when we are happy or in love, we can describe our hearts as 'singing' or 'buzzing'; or, at the other end of the spectrum, 'broken-hearted' describes the devastation we feel at having our hopes and dreams shattered. There's more to these metaphors than simply describing intense emotions: they point to the fascinating way our bodies experience these feelings, both emotionally and physically.

The association of the heart with emotion can be traced as far back as ancient Greek lyric poetry. Among the earliest known Greek examples, the sixth-century BC poet Sappho agonized over her own 'mad heart' quaking with love. Greek philosophers also agreed, more or less, that the heart was linked to our strongest emotions.

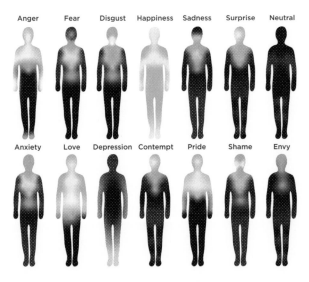

| Anger | Fear | Disgust | Happiness | Sadness | Surprise | Neutral |

| Anxiety | Love | Depression | Contempt | Pride | Shame | Envy |

Plato argued for the dominant role of the chest in love and in negative emotions of fear, anger, rage and pain. Aristotle expanded the role of the heart even further, granting it supremacy in all human processes.

Recent investigation has demonstrated this universal experience of emotion in the heart. In a study conducted in 2013 in Finland by researchers from Aalto University, University of Turku and University of Tampere, 700 individuals were asked to pinpoint where they felt different emotions in their bodies. The results were consistent and surprisingly similar across different cultures, with certain emotions such as anger, anxiety and fear strongly felt in the chest area, while happiness and love sparked activity all over the body. See the Bodily Map of Emotions above.

THE PHYSICAL HEART

This isn't to ignore the fact that the heart is a vitally important organ with its own biological functions, independent of emotions. The heart is central to human survival, pumping our blood and helping circulate oxygen throughout our bodies. Its health is therefore crucial. However, a growing body of research is demonstrating that 'heart-health' isn't just lowering your cholesterol and going for a run every day (although obviously these things help greatly!). An increasing amount of evidence is showing that our emotional state has a huge impact on our physical heart health.

Takotsubo cardio-myopathy, or 'broken-heart syndrome', was first described in Japan in 1990. It is when the left ventricle of the heart – its main pumping chamber – weakens and changes shape, usually as the result of severe emotional or physical stress, such as a sudden illness, the loss of a loved one, a serious accident, or a natural disaster such as an earthquake. The name 'takotsubo' is taken from the Japanese name for an octopus pot, which has a unique shape that the left ventricle comes to resemble. As a result of this shape change, the heart's ability to pump blood around the body is diminished, resulting in breathlessness, weakness and chest pain – similar to a heart attack, although upon examination doctors do not find any blocked arteries and are therefore usually at a loss to explain why the patient has these symptoms. Most people with takotsubo start a spontaneous process of recovery within hours or days, but it can take longer for the heart muscle to improve. Fatigue, chest pains and lack of energy are the most common continuing symptoms.

It's not just sudden distress that effects our hearts physically. Continued emotional stress causes a negative chain reaction in our bodies. Stress occurs when we perceive a threat to our existence or wellbeing. When we're angry, anxious, tense, frustrated, frightened or depressed, our body's natural response is to release hormones, including cortisol and adrenaline, which prepare the body to deal with stress. They cause our heart to beat more rapidly and our blood vessels to narrow, helping push blood to the centre of the body. These hormones also increase our blood pressure and blood sugar levels. As stress subsides, our blood pressure and heart rate should return to normal, though if we remain in a constant state of stress – perhaps due to a bad work environment, an unhealthy relationship or financial concerns – our hearts never get the chance to recover and remain in a state of 'fight or flight'. Sometimes we become so used to being in this state, that we don't even register it as unordinary.

LISTEN TO YOUR HEART

If ignoring our feelings can lead to long-term physical complications, then engaging with our hearts – both emotionally and physically – should be part of our daily routine. This section provides ways to optimize your relationship with your heart in both areas: from the quality of your emotional connections, to the daily buzz of your heart's vibrations. All the activities are designed with the aim of maximizing sensation in your heart (rather than just getting it to beat faster or slower). It's about feeling its warmth in your chest and reminding yourself to tune into what it's telling you.

LOVE YOURSELF

They say you can't love anyone until you love yourself, so let's start here.

Loving yourself can be a tricky concept to face. First, there's the fear that in doing so we are being vain or selfish. You might have been taught to put others first, and while this is an important philosophy that you shouldn't discard, there's a fine line between helping others and not caring for yourself because you are giving too much. In nursing and care roles, the priority is to look after yourself first. This might sound shocking as it contradicts the whole nature of the job, but if you aren't well yourself, how are you going to care for other people?

Second, during our lives we manage to accumulate a whole host of negative voices in our heads, which can sometimes be so

convincing that we start believing those voices are innately true and that we are unlovable. This is never the case. There is nothing in your head that hasn't been put there from an external source, so any negative beliefs you hold will always be based on something someone has said to you along the way. While criticism is admittedly unavoidable, remember that if it is not constructive, then it is uninformed, and therefore has no foundation. Put another way: if you know about something and you see someone doing it incorrectly, you don't put them down, you help them. If someone has put you down in the past and hasn't helped you find a way out, it's because they don't know what they are talking about and are merely trying to hide this by asserting themselves over you. Only listen to criticisms that are followed by solutions (and even then, if you don't like the solution, you can choose to ignore it!).

In learning to love yourself, you therefore need to work on two areas: defining your basic needs and boundaries, and controlling the negative voices in your head.

NEEDS AND BOUNDARIES

NEEDS.

'Self-care' is a term that gets used a lot and is often connected with either self-soothing during hard times, or self-indulgence during good times. Though both are important, self-care is much more mundane. It is the basic level of care and respect that you should give yourself every single day. It includes physical considerations – such as hygiene, diet and exercise – but also mental and emotional ones, such as taking breaks throughout the day and making sure you feel safe and supported.

Defining your basic needs is as simple as writing a list. Mentally, go through your day and write down what you need to feel healthy and happy. This should include:

- HYGIENE. Showering or bathing, brushing teeth, washing hair, shaving... What time of day? How often?

- DIET. Are you always forgetting to eat breakfast? Do you need to remind yourself to have fixed meal times rather than grazing through the day? Think also about the type of food that makes you feel healthy and fulfilled.

- EXERCISE. Do you need to fit a certain amount of walking into your day, or sports or gym time?

- HEALTH. Do you need to remember to take medication at certain times of the day? Supplements, vitamins, health foods etc.

- EMOTIONAL CONNECTION. How often do you need to see or talk to family and friends?

- SAFETY. Is there a certain route to work or to the shops that you feel safer taking, even if it's slightly longer? What makes you feel safe at home? This could be something as simple as a warm sweater and some soothing lighting. Do you need to divert more money towards being able to take taxis home late at night?

Once you have a list of everything you need, draw up a timetable of your week and work out how you will fit everything in. It might also be useful to work out a budget, if you realize you want to put more money towards certain needs. You don't have to stick to it, but getting it all down on paper and thinking practically about how much time and money you require for each aspect will make it easier to work your basic needs into every day, without lapsing.

BOUNDARIES.

Boundaries are limits you set for yourself, which tell others how they can treat you, what they can expect from you and how much you value yourself. Without them, you are exposed to vulnerability. People will take advantage of you if you let them: boundaries are a safety net to stop that from happening.

It's important that you have boundaries in place in all of your relationships, no matter how casual or serious, although setting them can be difficult if, while growing up, you have always been praised for acquiescing. If you're not sure whether you have weak boundaries, see if any of these questions ring true for you:

- Do you find it difficult to say no?
- Are you scared of not being liked?
- Do you agree to do things for other people, knowing that you don't really want to?
- Do you go out of your way to please people, with little appreciation in return?

If you answered 'yes' to any of these questions then, you've guessed it, you could do with building your boundaries up a little.

To find out where your boundaries lie, read through the list below and think of an example for each area where you have been made to feel uncomfortable in the past. That discomfort was your boundary being crossed. Make a note of it, and next time you find yourself in a similar situation, instead of making allowances, just politely shut down the conversation or walk away.

LIST OF BOUNDARIES

INTELLECTUAL: you are entitled to your own thoughts and opinions, as are others.

EMOTIONAL: you are entitled to your own feelings in a given situation, as are others.

PHYSICAL: you are entitled to your space, however wide it may be, as are others.

SOCIAL: you are entitled to your own friends and to pursuing your own social activities, as are others.

SPIRITUAL: you are entitled to your own spiritual beliefs, as are others.

GET THOSE NEGATIVE VOICES UNDER CONTROL

Tackling the problem of identifying and reining in the negative voices in our heads takes a bit more time than defining our basic needs. Many of these voices will be so intricately woven into our internal monologue that it can take some time to separate them out.

In order to confront and manage these negative thoughts, you first need to identify their source. This will involve a lot of paying attention to your instant mental responses (you could even call them reflexes) – those thoughts that erupt in reaction to something before you've had time to rationally consider them. An easy example would be someone inviting you to sing at a karaoke party and you immediately replying, "No, I can't sing". Can you really not sing, or were

you just told that once by a music teacher at school, and decided never to sing out loud again? What if this had never been said, and you had had the chance to develop your singing voice? On a deeper level, these responses can extend to things like our sense of intelligence, beauty and self-worth ("I'm too ugly/ boring for him/her."). Always, they are beliefs, not facts, and until you gain control of them, they will determine the course of your life.

HOW TO GET TO THE ROOT OF YOUR NEGATIVITY

OBSERVE YOUR RESPONSES.

Even the ones you don't say out loud. In particular, observe the responses that are based on negativity, prejudice and irrationality. One of the easiest ways to do this is to pay attention to what adjective you use most frequently after "I am not". I'm not funny, I'm not pretty, I'm not clever. Each time you hear one, make a note of it somewhere that you can refer back to regularly (keeping notes on your phone might be best). Keep adding each time you notice yourself making a negative response. The most common ones will rise to the top.

IDENTIFY THEIR SOURCE.

When you have a few, try and work out where they came from: a parent, a teacher, a sibling, a friend? Think back to that moment and try to put the comment into context. Was the person who said it ill-informed, angry, tired? Understand that it has a source and it isn't a universal truth, so that the next time you notice that thought rising, you can reason with it (and hopefully shut it down).

REMEMBER:
You are AMAZING!

NOURISH YOURSELF

We put our minds and bodies through a lot and they carry us as well as they can.

However, as with any beast of burden, if we want them to function at their best, they must be well nourished.

Think of nourishment as the best possible fuel you could give yourself – one which not only makes you run, but makes you glow while you're at it. Ultimately this depends on the quality of two things: nutrition and rest.

NUTRITION

Looking after your nutrition doesn't mean dieting. This isn't about restricting your intake, (unless you want or need to). You can still eat as much as you always do: just make sure that you are eating the best version of whatever you want to eat. Nourishment is about responding to and indulging the senses, and topping up on nutrients. When we do this, we generally have more energy and focus, our moods are more stable and we sleep better.

There are several ways you can maximize your nutrition:

BUY FRESH INGREDIENTS.

If you have the option of buying directly from a farmers' market rather than a supermarket, the produce will always be fresher, tastier and packed with more nutrients. Fruit and vegetables ripen on the branch or in the earth, rather than being harvested early and maturing in a shipping container, and animal products are generally from free-range, organic farms, where the animals have had better diets themselves. Although farmers' markets can often be more expensive than a supermarket for some items, a lot of the time they can be cheaper, especially if you are able to buy items individually rather than in multi-packs (as you often have to in the supermarket). There is also a lot of joy to be found in discovering new seasonal varieties, with their own unique colours, smells and tastes.

PAY ATTENTION TO YOUR CRAVINGS.

Cravings are incredibly important when it comes to nourishment. You must trust them! This is your body's way of telling you what it needs – although sometimes this might be encoded. For example, craving chocolate might be a sign that your body needs magnesium or iron (many women crave chocolate just before or during their periods, as the body relies on these nutrients during the first week of a cycle); or craving sugary, salty and fatty foods often means our bodies need more energy, either to fight stress or to combat sheer exhaustion. If this is the case, instead of reaching for the ice cream, try to have a few early nights, or practise meditation to manage your stress levels.

There will always be a story behind your cravings. Next time you have a really strong craving for something, try to decode it by googling what the main nutrient is in that food. If it's a constant craving, then make sure you are regularly eating foods that are rich in that nutrient, or consider taking a daily supplement. If taking supplements, always check first with your doctor that it is safe for you to do so.

START A FOOD DIARY.

Do you always go into a slump after eating meat? Or does coffee give you a headache, but you just can't resist it because you see it as a treat and it symbolizes taking a break? So many of us consume things daily which actually don't make us feel good at all, but we don't notice it because we aren't really paying attention to common patterns. Find out what gets you going versus what brings on the bloat by keeping a food diary for a couple of weeks. Chart energy levels, bloat levels, gassiness levels, sense of impending doom/optimism levels – you might be surprised by what this reveals!

REST

CREATE A RITUAL AROUND SLEEP.

Time spent sleeping is one of the most important parts of the day, but it can often be a source of great anxiety if you suffer from insomnia. So many factors affect our ability to sleep – and its quality once we're there. Incorporating some of the following elements into your bed-time ritual should help to improve your chances of a good sleep:

BREATHING. To get into a deep sleep, our brains need as much oxygen as they can get. Breathing through your nose, rather than your mouth, is one way to increase your oxygen intake. To get things going, take a few very deep inhalations through your nose once you've switched the lights out. To maximize the amount of oxygen getting into the blood stream – and bring down the amount of CO_2 – breathe in for three counts, hold for three, and breathe out for six (remember 3-3-6). This is also a good exercise to do if you wake in the night and struggle to get back to sleep.

RELAXING YOUR MUSCLES. It sounds obvious, but you'd be surprised how much tension you carry in your muscles, even in bed. Focus on really sinking every bone in your body into the mattress. Relax your face, your forehead, your jaw, your shoulders... You'll be closer to sleep within a few minutes.

SLEEP SUPPLEMENTS. Several nutrients are responsible for helping us sleep, and a deficiency in any of them will put you out of kilter. The main culprits are vitamin D, magnesium and calcium (your body needs both vitamin D and magnesium to absorb calcium, which produces melatonin and induces sleep). Herbally, valerian is commonly found in night-time teas and is usually effective, though it can leave you with a headache the next day. Sage is much cleaner and usually has no hangover. Make a tea with some fresh sage leaves, or take it in pill form just before switching the lights out. As always with supplements, discuss with a doctor whether they are safe for you to take – this might include requesting a blood test to see if you are deficient in anything.

ESSENTIAL OILS. The scent of certain plants has a calming effect on our nervous systems, so adding a few drops to your pillow or inhaling some from a tissue just before sleep can help you relax. Lavender is most commonly associated with bed-time, though you might prefer something else. Pay a trip to your local health food store and spend some time smelling a few different scents – buy the one you fall in love with.

FLYING PIGS. Finally – and slightly bizarrely – if you regularly struggle to switch your thoughts off and slip into a dreaming state, starting the dream consciously is an effective way of carrying your mind off to the land of nod.

If you're going round-and-round in circles thinking about work politics, imagine a few pigs flying through the office. It sounds mad, but by introducing something surreal, you are carrying your conscious thoughts towards the unconscious, and it's surprising how quickly your mind will cross over.

TREAT YOURSELF TO A REALLY GREAT BATH.

If waiting until night time for that sense of rest feels too far away, surrounding yourself with water is brilliant for both your head and your heart. As water tends to absorb our senses, visually and aurally, whether we are sitting by a lake, underneath a shower or soaking in a tub, it means that less stimulus is coming at us. As we focus on less externally, our minds can be more focused internally, which in turn results in our heart rates dropping and a sense of calm and clarity coming over us. Apparently, this is the reason why so many people have 'eureka' moments while in the bath or shower – their minds can focus on the problem they need to chew over.

Indulge yourself with a bath, but make it a really great one. Some of the following products could help with this:

- MAGNESIUM FLAKES. 100% magnesium. Fantastic for aching muscles, skin conditions like eczema, and helping the body and brain go into a state of deep relaxation.

- DEAD SEA SALTS. A real salt, with a mix of sodium chloride, magnesium, calcium, sulphur, bromide, zinc and potassium

- ESSENTIAL OILS. Eucalyptus, frankincense and lavender are some of the most soothing. Add a few drops to running water.

- SHAMPOOS, CONDITIONERS, BODY WASH. Think about investing in some really luxurious bath products that you only use every so often, when you really need a treat.

REMEMBER:

Nourishment is essential, not surplus. Don't feel guilty for looking after yourself.

ENHANCE YOUR CONNECTIONS

Healthy relationships are so important.

For over 80 years, Harvard University has been tracking the health and mental wellbeing of a group of 724 American men (and now their partners and children) as part of their Study of Adult Development. The findings were presented to the world by the study's current director, Robert J. Waldinger, in what is now one of the most watched TED Talks ever (*What Makes a Good Life? Lessons from the longest study on happiness*). Waldinger sums the key findings of the study up like this:

"The clearest message that we get from this 75-year study is this: good relationships keep us happier and healthier. Period."

Not wealth, not success, not the number of holidays you've had, but good relationships. However, it's not the number of relationships that matter, but the quality. You don't have to be at the centre of a big community, or a massive support system – obviously that helps, but ultimately you just need one or two very healthy, supportive relationships. As Waldinger goes on to explain:

"The experience of loneliness turns out to be toxic. People who are more isolated than they want to be from others, find that they are less happy, their health declines earlier in midlife, their brain functioning declines sooner, and they live shorter lives than people who are not lonely... And we know that you can be lonely in a crowd and you can be lonely in a marriage, so the second big lesson that we learned is that it's not just the number of friends that you have, and it's not whether you're in a committed relationship, but it's the quality of your close relationships that matters."

So, how do you maximize the quality of your relationships?

COMMUNICATE

The first step to making and getting the most out of anything is to understand it: communicate, learn, practise.

Misunderstandings can lead to upset, tension and anxiety. However, it can be hard to just casually open up a conversation about your deepest needs and feelings, even if it is with someone you're incredibly close to.

Using an existing and slightly playful structure can help remove the awkwardness around speaking about our emotions. One particularly useful approach can be found in *The 5 Love Languages*® – a book published by Gary Chapman in 1992, borne out of his counselling practice for married couples. The book focuses purely on marriage, though as a premise it can be applied to all relationships: friendships, romantic attachments, family relationships – in fact, if you have children in your life, one of the sweetest conversations you can have with them is finding out what their primary love language is.

It works around the idea that there are five ways that we all, as humans, communicate love. These include (see overleaf):

WORDS OF AFFIRMATION.

Complimenting, encouraging and uplifting your friend/partner/relative. Saying things like "You look fantastic" or "You were on such great form this evening – you had the whole room hanging on your every word!"

GIFTS.

These don't have to be expensive presents, but can include tokens as well, like some freshly picked flowers while out on a walk, or remembering what their favourite chocolate is and surprising them with it.

ACTS OF SERVICE.

Anything from cooking a meal for your friend/partner/child, to taking the rubbish bins out.

QUALITY TIME.

Giving your friend/partner/relative undivided attention. Going for a walk together, playing a game, or simply sitting and chatting.

PHYSICAL TOUCH.

Holding hands, hugging, kissing, giving a back rub, etc.

The idea is that we *all* communicate using *all* five love languages, but in different orders – and if we don't realize that our friend/partner/relative's *primary* love language is different to our own, then no matter how many flowers we pick on a walk round the park, if their primary love language is 'physical touch' and not 'gifts', then our expression of love will go unnoticed, and they will only feel put out that we haven't been linking arms with them as we walk around.

DISCOVER YOUR PRIMARY LOVE LANGUAGE

Sit down with your partner, friends and relatives, and find out what each other's primary love language is. You can discover your love language by:

TAKING AN ONLINE TEST.

If you google 'the 5 Love Languages', a free online test will pop up.

HAVE A DISCUSSION.

Simply talk through the list with your loved ones and work out which order you place each of the languages in. Be conscious of the fact that you will have different love languages for different types of love – for example, the way you express love romantically might be different to the way you express if platonically. Also, sometimes the way you give love isn't the same as the way you receive it, keep this in mind too, and work out your 'giving' and 'receiving' language for each person.

Once you have worked out the various love languages of your nearest and dearest, make sure that you practise engaging with each other in that language as often as you can. Be geeky and make a note of what each person's primary language is, so that when their birthday comes around, if you know they cherish quality time over gifts, perhaps you could plan a really personalized experience that maximizes the time you spend together, rather than buy them another plant pot.

GIVE

The second step in maximizing the quality of your relationships is to make sure they are mutually unconditional. This has to work both ways, though – the key word here is 'mutual'. Sometimes you can feel like you are giving so much that you are being taken from. Healthy relationships should not make either party feel exploited, unheard, anxious or diminished. If you feel this way in any of your relationships, check-in with the 'Boundaries' section in LOVE YOURSELF (page 64).

Giving unconditionally to a respectful and grateful 'receiver' can make you feel on top of the world. It makes you feel relevant and important, and enhances your sense of uniqueness.

Giving is a skill and, as with any skill, to develop your enjoyment of it, you need to practise. Volunteering is a fantastic way to remind yourself of the joys of giving – for both you and the recipient. You can do this on your own, or pair up with someone close to you, so that you can develop your own relationships while honing your understanding of the benefits of unconditional love.

TIPS FOR VOLUNTEERING

CHOOSE A CAUSE CLOSE TO YOUR HEART.

Even if it feels small and irrelevant compared to some of the big charity causes, everyone will benefit more if you are emotionally invested.

BE REALISTIC ABOUT WHAT YOU CAN CONTRIBUTE.

From the amount of time you can give to the types of skills you can offer. You might prefer to fundraise by doing a sponsored run, rather than volunteer weekly at a soup kitchen. Think about what you do best, and don't feel bad if you can only do it once a month/year.

START LOCALLY.

Small, local charities are usually in much greater need of support than the big national ones. See if there are any local causes that match with the area you want to volunteer in. Alongside being able to witness the personal impact of your giving more clearly, it will add to your sense of community and belonging.

REMEMBER.

It's all about the quality of your connections, not the quantity.

PORTRAITS

There's no better way to connect to someone you love than by really focusing on what it is that you love about them.

A portrait doesn't have to be a drawing. It could be a photograph, a collage or a piece of writing, even a song.

The main aim in creating a portrait is to capture the essence or the spirit of the person you are portraying. You're not trying to make them look like a famous portrait. Idiosyncrasies and mundane little details are key. That's not to say that you have to try and communicate a person's whole character in a brushstroke or a sentence – you might choose to make your portrait a specific memory rather than a character description – but just that it's important not to feel the weight of portrait history breathing down your neck. Be unique and personal.

Think about what it is that you associate with the sitter that you want the portrait to capture. It could be a favourite place, a smell (represented by a certain flower, tobacco, a perfume bottle), the way they dress, a meal you always share with them, a time of day that you associate with them. The best thing about portraiture is that it can be a composition of all these things. Spend some time gathering the parts of your portrait. Write down a minimum of five key qualities or memories that you want to include in your portrait.

If you can spend time with the subject

of your portrait, do so. Ask them for their own interpretations of the key qualities or memories that you've chosen. If they're willing to sit for the portrait, fantastic! The conversations that will emerge during the sitting will only serve to strengthen your bond. If you're based in different cities or countries, think about whether or not you'd like to study them via video call or, if you find it easier working from a photo, maybe you could chat to them on the phone while you're working.

Now that you have an outline for the content, decide what medium you'd like to create your portrait in. If this is your first portrait, choose something you're comfortable with: don't put too much pressure on your technical skills. The list below provides some ideas for what is best depending on what your end goal is.

PAINTING.

Brilliant for capturing colour, movement and energy. Also good for arranging a composition of several parts and bringing it altogether as a single entity without it looking forced. Be confident in your style – the more you can see your hand in the work, the more personal the finished piece will be.

PHOTOGRAPHY.

Perfect for creating an accurate representation of someone. Play around with lighting, setting and clothing to make the message of your portrait more defined. Just because a photo can be taken in an instant doesn't mean you can't take your time bringing it together.

COLLAGE.

Fantastic for portraying a person's wider world. Incorporate photos, news clippings, illustrations, pieces of text.

DRAWING.

As with painting, a brilliant way for your own hand and style to have a presence alongside the representation of the person you are drawing. Don't try to create a pencil drawing that looks like a black-and-white photograph of someone (i.e. all the same tone and depth) – use darker lines to outline and highlight their strongest features, or to accentuate the movement of their hair, or to emphasize their shadows.

SCULPTURE.

A great way of bringing a physical presence into the room. Depending on your experience, this can be a rudimentary or even an abstract form – emphasizing the outline of their face, or the hollows of their bone structure – or it can be precise, using exact measurements and creating life-like features to replicate them in 3D.

WRITING.

A favourite memory, an irritating but endearing quirk, a precise description of the person's appearance… build an image using language. Take some time choosing your words and use similes to evoke sensations linked to the sitter.

MAKING MUSIC.

If you're musically gifted, you could try capturing your sitter in a song. What do they sound like? What is their rhythm? What instruments represent them? Take some time getting to know their favourite music before you start composing, and see if you can work this in to your piece too.

REMEMBER.

Make it personal, from your style to the subject matter. Don't try and emulate, otherwise the portrait loses its original connection.

LOVE LETTERS

We're used to thinking of love letters as romantic declarations, created in moments of passion, obsession and longing.

But there are so many different types of love, and the focus of love letters doesn't need to be limited to desire.

It might sound mad (or vain), but asking your friends and family to send you some love letters is a fantastic way to surround yourself with some love and appreciation – and, of course, to return the sentiment in your own love letter to them. You don't need to call it a love letter directly: you could suggest that you both send each other a short letter with a favourite memory included, plus a line about what you love about each other.

If the thought of asking someone to write you a love letter makes you cringe, a really good alternative it to write yourself one. And no, it's not tragic! Writing a love letter to yourself is fascinating because you *really* know yourself. You know how your mind works, you know all your habits, you know your strengths and your weaknesses. You can really be honest about what you love. Maybe you love that you're irrational or impulsive, or creative (even if you never do anything about it). You can praise all the parts of you that no-one ever sees; all the bits that you keep to yourself, because maybe they're a bit weird, but that you love nonetheless. Whatever it is, ignore the outside world and any negative voices that tell you you're 'too this' or 'not enough that'. You're alone in your room. What do you love? It will be the most intimate and honest love letter you'll ever receive.

HOW TO SEND AND RECEIVE A GREAT LOVE LETTER

BACK UP YOUR AFFECTION WITH SPECIFIC MEMORIES. As lovely as it is to receive a letter full of gushy adjectives, if the words aren't linked to concrete evidence, it can feel a little like the author has just flicked through the thesaurus without much personal connection to you. Use specific memories to illustrate why you love the reader so much, so that there's no doubt this letter is based solely on them.

BE GENUINE. Don't use fancy language and don't use humour to cover up your affection. Write the letter as you would speak it if the reader was in front of you.

SEND/REQUEST LOVE WHERE IT'S MOST NEEDED. Identify if there are any insecurities that need addressing and send or request some love in this particular area. It will make your letter all the more pertinent and appreciated.

CARRY YOUR LOVE ON INTO THE FUTURE. Finish all your love letters by saying what you hope the running theme of the reader's life will be. With any love letter, it's likely that the recipient will read it again and again over the years (even if this is you!), so including a wish for the future is a great way of creating a sense of continued and everlasting love.

REMEMBER.

Everyone loves a love letter. Don't be afraid to suggest this to your friends.

SING

The benefits of singing are almost countless.

Psychologically and emotionally, when we sing we release endorphins, the feel-good brain chemical that makes you feel uplifted and happy; it lowers our stress levels and it improves mental alertness. Socially (if singing as part of a group), it can broaden our circle of friends, boost confidence and improve communication skills. And not forgetting its physical benefits, which range from exercising our lungs and improving posture to apparently even boosting our immune systems.

Science aside, there's also that incredible feeling you get in your chest when you really sing your heart out: the vibration that rumbles up through your throat, around your whole ribcage and stirs the heart.

WHAT TO DO

GOING SOLO.

If you're going at this on your own, then you can sing anytime, anywhere:

AT HOME. Turn the music up when you're home alone and go for it – or if you feel self-conscious about hearing your voice wobble or not hitting the notes bang on, put some headphones on to drown out the sounds and sing at the top of your voice.

SINGING LESSONS. Use this as an opportunity to really develop your vocal chords and improve your technique. Have a google of local singing teachers, or check local noticeboards in schools, churches, universities, etc. If you prefer to learn from the comfort of your own home and are happy to learn over video call, there are so many online singing tutors, some with free trials.

BE PART OF A CROWD.

GET SOME FRIENDS ROUND AND SING KARAOKE. There are lots of free karaoke songs on YouTube, or just put your favourite hits on and belt them out together. Alternatively, look for a karaoke set which lets you turn your TV, laptop or tablet into a karaoke machine, with thousands of songs to stream from a website or app (such as Lucky Voice).

JOIN A CHOIR. If you live in a city, it's likely there are choirs nearby just waiting for you to find them via an online search. Some will be free; others will be paying. Most will offer free taster sessions, so go along to a few and see which you like best. Think about what type of music you want to sing – choirs don't just sing hymns.

START YOUR OWN CHOIR. If you can't find what you're looking for, why not start your own choir? It doesn't have to be big – just three or four singers is enough to get going with. Ask friends, coworkers or family if they'd like to join, or post an announcement on a local neighbourhood website. You'll likely find singers and musicians who have been waiting for someone to suggest it. You can download free sheet music online, from sites like 8notes.com; and if you're looking for a rehearsal space, try local schools, universities, churches, etc.

REMEMBER.

This doesn't have to be about being the next Pavarotti; this is about opening your lungs and heart. If singing isn't your thing, humming or chanting will work as well. Anything, as long as you feel those vibrations.

DANCE

Dancing is a fantastic way to connect with our bodies – and to remember that we have them.

Although it's a form of exercise, and so brings all the benefits of other cardio activities with it, dancing is different because to a degree it is intrinsic. Children start dancing without being told how to; even animals dance. There's something about it that doesn't require too much thought – you just start moving and your body seems to know how to keep going.

Dancing is also irrefutably linked to how we're feeling. At some point in our lives, we'll all have said "I don't feel like dancing" in response to an invitation to get up and bust a groove. We might have been too tired, too stressed, too heartbroken... but if whoever extended

the invitation manged to convince us to ignore that and just dance for a few minutes, it's likely that we all felt better by the end of it.

There are two types of dancing. There's the unregulated, unguarded, slightly-mad-just-going-for-it-type, with no rhyme, reason or preparation: you just let your body move in whatever way it wants to. Then there's the structured, focused dance routine or performance piece. Both are brilliant.

One of my favourite facts about the first type of dance (going for it on your own, rather than following a set routine) is that it exploded at the same time as the invention of the vinyl record player. People could suddenly listen to music in their own homes – or rather their own rooms – and so started dancing on their own. When they then made it into the clubs to dance with friends, they already knew what they wanted to do, and so the formal dance disintegrated into the informal: a room full of people shaking in time to the music in their own way.

That's not to say that the more structured style of dance isn't equally as popular: from ballet to ballroom, the constant demand for these types of dance – both in terms of classes and performances – solidifies our obsession with them. Learning to dance as a discipline is fantastic for your focus, concentration, spatial awareness and (if part of a duo or a troupe) your sense of teamwork.

Many forms of dancing, such as ballroom, are appropriate for people with limited mobility or chronic health issues. All types of dance boost our energy, happiness and self-esteem. Let's dance!

DANCING ALONE

MAKE THE MOST OF BEING HOME ALONE.

We've all done it, and it's often the best feeling in the world. Very little instruction needed here, other than clear some floor space, turn up the music and go for it. Dress up if you feel like it, or wear gym clothes if you know you're going to get hot and sweaty. Pull the curtains or not – this moment is entirely your own.

FOLLOW A DANCE TUTORIAL.

Learning a dance routine is a fantastic focus when you need some distraction from other thoughts, not to mention a great provider of a sense of progress and achievement. There are hundreds of tutorials on YouTube: take your pick from a variety of instructors showing you a multitude of different types of dance.

TWO'S COMPANY, THREE'S A CROWD

PARTNER UP.

There are so many different dances that you can do in a pair, but a ballroom dance class is a good place to start as it covers a multitude of dance styles, including the waltz, tango, foxtrot, quickstep, samba, cha-cha and rumba, to name a few. You don't have to have an existing partner in order to learn how to ballroom dance. Dance classes are extremely welcoming and dancers normally rotate around the room, so that you become used to dancing with a variety of different people. Wear loose-fitting, breathable clothes that don't restrict your movements while you're learning and practising, and make sure you have a low-heeled shoe – a suede-soled dance

shoe is best, though perhaps wait until you know you're serious before investing in a pair.

BE PART OF A CROWD.

There's a huge amount of satisfaction to be had from moving in perfect sync with a bunch of other people. This could be anything from joining a group class to forming your own dance crew. Different to dancing with a partner, being part of a group can take the pressure off slightly if you prefer to slip into the background, while keeping that sense of team spirit. From ballet to jazz, hip-hop to dancehall, try a few classes and see what suits your sense of rhythm best.

REMEMBER.

Let go of insecurity and fear – regardless of your level. The sooner you stop worrying about what you look like, the sooner your body can relax and move properly and your heart can start buzzing.

LAUGH

There's a good reason why TV sitcoms use laughter tracks: laughing is contagious.

And the more laughter you bring into your own life, the happier and more fulfilled your heart and the hearts of those around you will feel.

Laughter creates strong emotional bonds. How many friendships and relationships have been formed on the basis that you 'just didn't stop laughing'? A good bout of laughter often feels like a day in the sunshine, and in fact the physical benefits are almost identical: laughter strengthens your immune system, boosts mood, diminishes pain and protects you from the damaging effects of stress. On top of this, laughing is a great cardio workout, especially for those who are incapable of doing other physical activity due to injury or illness. It gets your heart pumping and burns a similar amount of calories per hour as walking at a slow to moderate pace (though admittedly you'd have to laugh continuously for quite a while before you start burning those pounds...).

A bit like dancing, laughter is intrinsic to us as human beings. Babies start laughing out loud from as young as three or four months old, long before there's any chance of developing a sense of humour. Laughter is not only a basic human response, but also a fundamental experience, and aiming to bring laughter into your life daily is a guaranteed way to uplift your heart and make it bubble.

A FEW WAYS TO BRING SOME LAUGHTER HOME

SPEND TIME WITH FUN, PLAYFUL PEOPLE.

People who laugh easily – both at themselves and at life's absurdities – are routinely able to find humour in the most mundane things. Their playful point of view and laughter are contagious. Even if you don't consider yourself a light-hearted, humorous person, you can still seek out people who like to laugh and make others laugh, and see how catching their way of looking at the world is.

BRING HUMOUR INTO CONVERSATIONS.

There's nothing like discussing your most embarrassing moments with friends to get those crying-with-laughter tears rolling. Or, if this feels too much like exposing

yourself, start with a less scary question, such as "What's the funniest thing that happened to you today? This week? In your life?".

WATCH SOME COMEDY. SIMPLE BUT EFFECTIVE!

This could be your favourite funny movie, sitcom or stand-up comedy. This could be your favourite funny movie, sitcom or stand-up comedy – perhaps even a live performance. While the big name comedians can be expensive to see in real life, local comedy is just as good, and even if it's terrible, it can be hilarious if you're with a good group of friends.

DO SOME LAUGHTER YOGA.

Fake it until you make it! Laughter yoga is based on the idea that as long as you are laughing – even if it's fake – your body will not recognize the difference and you will reap all the benefits of real laughter. Through a combination of simple yoga breathing techniques and laughter meditation, even though it might feel weird to start with, you'll be surprised how quickly the laughter catches. Do a search to see if there are any classes near you, or try a tutorial out on YouTube. Alternatively, if you want to start your own laughter club with some friends, try the six exercises below:

1. GREETING LAUGHTER.
   Walk around the space you are in, with palms pressed together at the upper chest in the Namaste greeting. When you pass another person in your group, look into each other's eyes and laugh together.

2. LION LAUGHTER.
   Thrust out the tongue, widen the eyes and stretch the hands out like claws while laughing.

3. HUMMING LAUGHTER.
   Laugh with the mouth closed and hum.

4. SILENT LAUGHTER.
   Open your mouth wide and laugh without making a sound. Look into other people's eyes and make funny gestures.

5. GRADIENT LAUGHTER.
   Start by smiling and then slowly begin to laugh with a gentle chuckle. Increase the intensity of the laugh until you've achieved a hearty laugh. Then gradually bring the laugh down to a smile again.

6. HEART-TO-HEART LAUGHTER. Move close to a person and hold each other's hands and laugh.

REMEMBER.

Laughter is innate. Don't try to over-rationalize it. Just enjoy it.

LISTEN TO YOUR FAVOURITE TUNES

It might feel a bit simple to be told to listen to your favourite music – no doubt you are already doing this any time you listen to music.

But how often do you do it as an active intention, knowing you are going to choose songs that will make your heart skip, and that the music will be your sole focus for however long you can give it, rather than just background music while you work or hang out with friends?

Studies have shown that music can boost our mood and fend off depression. It can apparently also improve blood flow in ways similar to statins, lowering levels of stress-related hormones like cortisol and easing pain. One study even found that listening to music before an operation can improve post-surgery outcomes by reducing anxiety and subsequently aiding the healing process.

As with all other forms of art, don't give in to pressure about what you should or shouldn't be listening to. Some people might find Mozart aggravatingly dull and rock metal soothing, while others might find that sixteenth-century lute music really solves all their problems. If it makes your heart sing, tune in.

Whatever it is that gets you going, try to listen intentionally for a set amount of time each day, so that you'll be able to notice if it makes a difference to the way you approach things.

WAYS TO MAKE THIS MORE FUN

ASK FRIENDS FOR SONGS THAT REMIND THEM OF YOU.

These will likely be attached to shared memories of trips, parties, school... This is different to asking friends to make you an entirely new playlist, because you know you already love these songs. Get your friends to make one suggestion each, and then make your own playlist out of all of them.

BE CHRONOLOGICAL.

We have memories attached to songs, but we also have songs attached to memories. It's rare that just one song will remind us of a time in our lives. Create some playlists that are linked to points in your life, like your last school year or first year of parenthood.

PLAN AHEAD.

Music is fantastic at lifting our spirits, but sometimes when you're in need of a boost, you find that you've forgotten every happy song you know. Plan ahead for yourself, and any time you come across a tune that makes you feel amazing, add it to a 'Happy' or even an 'Emergency' playlist.

BUY GOOD SPEAKERS OR HEADPHONES.

Invest in the best quality you can afford. It will be a gift to yourself that really keeps on giving.

GO AND SEE THEM LIVE.

There's nothing like being part of a crowd, sharing the love and the acoustics of your favourite band or orchestra. Even if you have to travel to another city, live performances always leave you buzzing. If you have the time and budget, make this a regular outing to top up your listening at home.

REMEMBER.
Get that Guilty Pleasures playlist on!

ENJOY NATURE

The heart swells when all the senses are engaged.

Spending some time in nature – whether it's sitting in your garden and listening to the birds sing, walking through a forest, or white water rafting through a ravine – provides an opportunity for your whole body to immerse itself in its surroundings and absorb some natural goodness.

The physical benefits of spending time in nature range from lowering stress levels, to increasing production of vitamin D (responsible for healthy bones, good sleep and stabilizing your mood), to strengthening the immune system and improving memory. All these things will happen naturally as you move through nature. To absorb the heart, though, you will need to engage

on a more detailed level, bringing your thoughts and attention to everything around you.

Build a good chunk of time into your week when you can interact with nature in some way. Focus on immersing the senses, keeping a journal of what you notice on each outing, so that at the end of the year you'll have a heady, seasonal, sensory souvenir.

IMMERSE THE SENSES

SIGHT.

Observe as much as you can. This could be noticing the variance in plants around you or watching bees as they collect pollen. To take your level of 'seeing' up a notch, stop and make a drawing or a painting of what you're looking at, or take a photo. Try to learn something about the different flora and fauna around you, for example which leaves go with which bark?

SOUND.

Close your eyes and listen to birdsong, the sound of wind through the trees, the bees and insects buzzing around. If it's winter, listen to the stillness – how sound cuts through the cold more sharply. Notice how much is happening, and how much action there is, in every moment.

SMELL.

From the scent of flowers in spring to the earthy smell that comes just after the rain, again close your eyes and focus on the aromas around you. Notice how the time of day, the temperature and the season effect things.

TASTE.

There's nothing like the taste of something freshly picked, though stick to what you know and don't take any guesses. Think of fruit: apples, plums, pears; flowers: honeysuckle, jasmine, lavender; and herbs: mint, basil, rosemary.

TOUCH.

Reach out and touch things! Leaves, bark, grass, flowers, soil. Take your shoes off and feel the grass or the sand under your feet. If you're by a river or the sea, stick your hands in. Wash your face in it. Don't leave without having physically interacted with your surroundings.

REMEMBER.

Pay attention. Nature can reveal valuable metaphors for our own lives. For example, the renewal of life every year reminds us that even in the depths of winter, growth is happening beneath the surface, and that seeds laid down months before will blossom.

TIDY	MESSY
MAKE BASKETS	PRINT
MAKE MUSIC	GARDEN
SEW	WORK WITH CLAY
KNIT (OR CROCHET)	BAKE
MACRAMÉ	EXERCISE

HANDS

There is a sort of chicken-and-egg debate going on among bio-archaeologists. It is around the question of what came first: the human hand or the tool?

The reason that the answer isn't clearer is because the development of stone tools is so synonymous with the development of the hand. We have been making from the word 'go', and our mental and emotional states are all wrapped up together with this specific aspect of our physical development.

THE PHYSICAL HAND

While a history of the human hand might not sound like a barrel of laughs, understanding just how incredible our hands are will make you appreciate them – and hopefully use them – more.

A hand is a *prehensile*, which means that as an organ (yup, it's an organ!) it is has adapted to grasp and hold things. The word is derived from the Latin term *prehendere*, meaning 'to grasp'. There are 29 major and minor bones, 29 major joints, at least 123 named ligaments, 35 muscles, and 48 named nerves in your hand – all working to help us hold, grasp and manipulate things. The whole hand is covered by papillary ridges (a.k.a. fingerprints), which act as friction pads.

While many other mammals and primates have hands that grasp, none are as dextrous as human hands. This is due to the strength of the connections between our hands and the neurons in the region of the brain involved in the planning, control and execution of voluntary movements (the motor cortex), as well as motor neurons in our spinal cord. In other words, our hands are able to do all the wonderful things they can do because they are more connected to the brain than in other species. Our hands are direct tools of our consciousness.

They are also the main source of differentiated tactile sensations: there are around 17,000 touch receptors and free nerve endings in the palm alone. Perhaps it is for this reason that we love holding hands – it activates all these thousands of nerve endings. Holding hands is just one of many gestures that we make with our hands, that allow us to express our personalities and feelings. From waving excitedly at a friend as we approach them, to judging a coworker by the strength (or weakness) of a handshake, we

communicate daily with our hands.

And last but not least, of course, we use our hands to create. We make life easier, more enjoyable, more attractive, tastier, more expansive and safer with our hands. We build shelter and we defend with them; we clothe and decorate; we source and prepare food; and, of course, we eat and drink with them. The majority of our physical interactions with the world involve our hands.

THE MENTAL HAND

Our hands also have a direct correlation with our mental wellbeing. In contemporary Western society, we view prosperity as being surrounded with creature comforts and personal services: the less physical effort or exertion needed, the better. Yet this may be suffocating our neural functions. At the University of Richmond, Dr. Kelly Lambert explored the relationship between hand use, current cultural habits and mood. She found that hands-on work satisfies our primal need to make things and can also boost our energy and contentedness. Too much time spent on technological devices, coupled with the fact that we buy almost all of what we need rather than having to make it, has deprived us of processes that provide pleasure, meaning and real pride.

Hand activity – from knitting or woodwork, to growing vegetables or chopping them – has been proven to lower stress, relieve anxiety and modify depression. There is value in the routine action, the mental rest and focus, and the purposeful creative, domestic or practical endeavour. Functioning hands also foster a flow in the mind that leads to spontaneous joyful and creative thought. Peak moments often occur as we putter and ponder.

The tragedy, however, is that we are increasingly denying ourselves these moments. 'We just sit there and we press buttons', Dr Lambert states, commenting on a typical 'work' scenario for most people. 'We start to lose a sense of control over our environment.' Matthew Crawford, author of *The Case for Working with Your Hands: Or Why Office Work is Bad for Us and Fixing Things Feels Good*, agrees with this theory that a lack of interaction with the physical world destroys our sense of responsibility and control over it. In his TEDx talk 'Intellectual Competence', he remarks on how, with fewer occasions to be directly responsible for your own physical environment, the modern personality is getting reformed in the direction of passivity and dependence. This is destructive, because it is not in our nature to behave this way. 'It's a rare person who is naturally inclined to sit still for 16 years at school, and then indefinitely at work', he states.

If working with our hands is a fundamental part of human behaviour and development, then the more we fail to use our hands, the more we are limiting our development. What would happen if we started to pick things up again? The next few pages will help you find out.

MAKE BASKETS

Crafting your own basket is one of the most satisfying and empowering things you can do.

In making something so beautiful from something as basic as reed or willow, all your creative and intellectual faculties are engaged, as well as your practical capabilities. It sounds strange, but it makes you feel like a real human. The sensation of bending branches to your will and creating something useful reminds us that we are inventive and intelligent beings.

It also leaves you with a much deeper connection to the landscape. Even in the winter, you will start to see the barren branches of a tree as an exciting resource, rather than a reminder of the cold. Start with a simple basket and see how you get on. If it grabs you, you can go on to make all sorts of things, from pet baskets to laundry baskets to beach bags!

HOW TO MAKE YOUR OWN BASKET

TOOLS.

Only a few simple tools are needed for basket weaving:

GOOD STRONG SCISSORS AND A SHARP KNIFE, for cutting and pointing the branches.

A PAIR OF ROUND-NOSED PLIERS are valuable for kinking the stakes before bending them, particularly when the angle has to be sharp.

A BODKIN (a pointed metal tool in a wooden handle) is very helpful, both for making an opening when weaving branches through each other, and for pushing a rod in position after the gap has been made. However, if you're just starting out, a screwdriver or a good strong knitting needle can also work.

MATERIALS

Although you can work with many different types of cane, reed and grass, an easy material to start off with is willow, as it is naturally very supple and therefore easy to manipulate without snapping (too often).

WHERE TO SOURCE YOUR WILLOW.

The three most commonly used types of willow for weaving are *Salix purpurea*, *Salix viminalis* and *Salix triandra* (*Salix* is the Latin name for willow). You can buy these types of willow online, with rods already cut and dried, in a variety of weights and colours – from beautiful gleaming white to golden tan, from red to a rich dark brown.

Rods can come either with the bark stripped off (buff) or with the bark left on (brown). The difference here is both in aesthetics and toughness to weave. If you are new to weaving and/or don't have much hand strength, then it is best to start with buff willow as it's much easier to work. Green willow refers to undried willow that in theory could sprout life again if stuck in the ground. If you weave a basket from willow straight off the tree (green) it will shrink as it dries, distorting your basket's shape. For this reason, it's best to work with willow that has been dried and then re-soaked, as it has been pre-shrunk.

SIZE.

Rods can be bought in bundles known as 'bolts' sized from 1m (3 feet) long up to 2.7m (9 feet) long. You will need about 70 rods to make a simple round basket.

To determine how long the rods should be for a particular basket-weaving project, multiply the desired diameter of your basket by three, and then add a little extra for safety (it's better to have too much and trim down, than too little!). So, for a basket with a diameter of 30cm (12in), you will need rods slightly longer than 1m (3 feet) in length; for a basket with a diameter of 60cm (2 feet), you will need rods around 2m (6 feet) in length.

SOAKING YOUR WILLOW.

You will not be able to weave a basket with dried willow, as it will simply snap. The re-soaking of the dried willow makes it pliable again. When your willow arrives, you will need to soak it, either in a bath-tub or a paddling pool, and then wrap in a damp cloth. Different willows have different soaking times. You will be able to find out how much time you need to soak your willow for from the retailer or the packaging.

ANATOMY OF A ROD.

You will notice that the rod is thicker at the base end (the end that was closest to the ground when it was growing). This is known as the butt. The topmost, thin end is known as the tip. Rods have a natural curve to them: the inside curve is known as the belly; the outer curve is the back. When weaving, work with the natural shape of the rod so that you don't bend it at an unnatural angle to itself, causing it to snap.

WHAT TO DO

Though not impossible to weave a basket using written instructions, if this is your first go, it's often easier to watch-and-learn. As such, online tutorials are the best place to start. HANNA VAN AELST (www.hannavanaelst. com) is a basket-maker and artist based in Ireland, who has put together a fantastic free online course for beginners in basket-making.

Alternatively, there are lots of tutorials on YouTube, some more eccentric than others! Have a search, or if you'd prefer to learn in person, see if there are any basket-making courses near you.

REMEMBER.

Always soak your rods for the full amount of time, even if it's tempting to cut this short, otherwise they will kink or snap and your basket will be ruined.

MAKE MUSIC

Making music is a bit like starting a fire. With just hands, breath and a few raw materials, we ignite something extraordinary.

It's often said that music picks up where words leave off – that making music is a way of expressing an emotion or feeling that can't be explained. What's remarkable, though, is that these non-verbal expressions can often be instantly understood by whoever is listening. It turns out that our language extends beyond words, and includes tones, pitches and beats. Maria von Trapp (yes, the real one) famously called music a "mighty weapon", succeeding when rationality fails in breaking through to a person's raw humanity. "Music acts like a magic key," she said, "to which the most tightly closed heart opens."

Music also manages to distil our experiences, making even the most uncomfortable emotions digestible. Alsatian polymath Albert Schweitzer noticed how music could soothe us even when its focus was a scary or negative one: "Joy, sorrow, tears, lamentation, laughter – to all these music gives voice, but in such a way that we are transported from the world of unrest to a world of peace, and see reality in a new way." Playing an instrument is a fantastic way of broadening our resources for self-expression, as well as helping us understand the sounds and movements of our experiences.

Then there's the physical joy of it: the feeling of your hands stretching across the keys of a piano, the strange pleasure found in the hardening of your fingertips over time from plucking at guitar strings, or experiencing the real strength of your lungs and diaphragm as you breathe life into a wind instrument. In a world where the majority of us have very little physical engagement with our work, witnessing the power of our hands, fingertips and lungs can be invigorating.

(Re-)engage with this magical ability of your hands to turn feelings into sounds by picking up an instrument. Even if you've never played a musical instrument in your life, you can do this. As always, make it fun. Put away thoughts and fears around whether you can or can't (you can!) and whether it sounds any good. Everything is achievable with practice.

CHOOSING YOUR INSTRUMENT

Regardless of whether or not you already play an instrument, have a think about whether there's one in particular that you want to try out. Perhaps something you always wanted to play as a child, but your parents wouldn't let you because it was too noisy, or not traditional enough?

Extend this to the type of music you want to learn too: pop, jazz, rock, folk – it doesn't always have to be Beethoven. Who's your favourite artist and what song do you listen to on repeat? Can you get sheet music for it? Or try and mimic it by ear, teaching yourself a new way of playing? Discover some new tunes by spending some time going through playlists that match the type of music you want to play (e.g. 'most romantic piano music' or 'rock ballads').

SIGHT VS. SOUND

If you're starting this completely from scratch, you'll need to work out if you learn better by sight or by sound. The ability to read music from a score seems to come more easily to some than others, while some people find that they're able to mimic note for note a tune that they've just heard. With either method, if you're serious, you'll need help from a tutor. Think about whether you want to invest in music lessons properly, or if this feels too much of a leap, do you have a friend or coworker who could teach you the basics (perhaps you could do a skills swap and teach them something in return)? Alternatively, you may be able to find free online tutorials: www.skillshare.com and www.youcanplayit.com are two good places to start, although have a search for your specific needs and see what comes up.

GOOD INSTRUMENTS FOR COMPLETE BEGINNERS

A BUCKET!

If you've always had a great sense of rhythm but the thought of investing in a drum kit feels too extravagant, get to know the basics on an upturned bucket or some pots and pans at home – www.bucketdrumming.net is a great resource for learning essential rhythms, as well as more complex headline hits. Membership is free – though you can upgrade to a paid plan as you become more involved.

UKULELE.

Inexpensive to buy and super fun to play, the ukulele is one of the easiest instruments to learn. With just four nylon strings (instead of the guitar's six), you can quickly pick up simple chords and play some of your favourite songs in just a few weeks.

You'll also be able to gain many fundamental skills that make it easier if you ever want to graduate from the ukulele to the guitar.

HARMONICA.

Be it blues, jazz, rock, folk or country music, the harmonica (also known as the 'blues harp') is a great choice for adult beginners. You don't need to know a lot in order to start playing and its biggest advantage is that any note will be 'in key' — it's hard to sound bad on harmonica! Plus, as harmonicas are very portable, you can carry and practise it anywhere, anytime. There are some good beginner tutorials at www.youcanplayit.com

PIANO.

The piano may seem complex — after all, you need to coordinate both hands at once — but it's one of the easiest instruments for adults to learn. Because the notes are all laid out in front of you, it's easier to understand than many other instruments.

RECORDER.

A familiar instrument from most of our childhoods for the simple reason that it's very easy to learn. There are five types of recorder: sopranino, soprano (also known as descant and the one you will most likely have played at school) alto, tenor and bass. All are a good base for learning more complex wind instruments, such as the saxophone, oboe, clarinet or bassoon. You'll find music and tutorials at www. youcanplayit.com. This is a great instrument to learn in duet with a friend.

REMEMBER.

This isn't about becoming the world's best concert pianist (although well done if you do!). It's about the joy of using your hands to make a sound and express a feeling. Have fun with it.

SEW

Whether it's a cushion cover (pillow), a make-up bag, a shirt or a dress, it's hard to top the feeling that comes with answering "I made it myself", when asked where you got something.

Sewing is a fascinating occupation for your hands and your mind. You learn how things fit together; you get to know the different weights and textures of fabrics, and how to tell their composition based on their lustre and sheen; you explore how different materials interact; and you feel the tension in a thread as it brings two pieces of fabric together.

And it isn't just manual or tactile joys that sewing brings: there are the creative delights too. Being able to perfectly match a colour, a shape or a design to a friend – summing up their energy and personality in an object or a garment – is a beautiful gift.

If you've never sewn before, you don't need to go out and buy a sewing machine to get started. Sewing by hand is just as effective and can be even more enjoyable than sewing with a machine. The sensation of bringing two pieces of fabric together between your hands, as you stitch, feels slightly godly. It also allows you to control tension, and you will get to know how the fabric works more intimately.

MAKE A CUSHION COVER

An easy piece to start with – that will allow you to experience all the highs of sewing – is a cushion (pillow) cover. Even if you're a pro-sewer, new cushion covers are always a satisfying way to re-energize an interior, or make as a personal gift to a friend. The instructions below are for an envelope cushion cover, which means you insert the cushion through an opening at the back, with no need for a zipper.

To get the greatest sense of pride out of your cushion cover, splash out on the fabric. The general rule when makers price their pieces for sale is to triple the cost of the materials, so that they cover the fabric, their labour and make a profit. So if you put the labour in for free and forget about the profit, you'll end up with a high-end cushion for a fraction of the shop price. That feels pretty good!

BASIC TERMS.

Before we get started, the following terms will help you understand the instructions:

RIGHT SIDE. The outer face of the fabric (the side you want to see).

WRONG SIDE. The inside of the fabric (the side you don't want to see).

TENSION. The tightness of the stitch. Different fabrics can withstand different tensions.

SEAM ALLOWANCE. The distance between the edge of the fabric and your line of stitching. As a standard, this is always 1.5cm (⅝in).

RAW EDGE. Any unsewn edge of fabric.

WHAT YOU NEED.

- 1M (1 YARD) FABRIC – choose a heavy cotton or linen
- SCISSORS. If you are a beginner, you can use the 'normal' scissors that you would use for cutting paper. As you progress, though, you will need to invest in a pair of sewing scissors (usually 20-cm/8-in

blades). Sewing scissors are different to normal scissors as they are angled to cut parallel to the surface that the fabric is sitting on, so that you can cut straight. Never use your fabric scissors to cut paper as this will blunt the blades.

- SEWING PINS. If you have a choice, get the ball-head pins, as they are easier to use and to see.
- A NEEDLE OR A SEWING MACHINE.
- THREAD. Use a cotton thread if you are sewing cotton or silk; and a polyester thread for man-made fabrics.
- A TAPE MEASURE. A soft tape measure is best (rather than the solid tape measures that you use for DIY) as it will be able to bend around the curves of the cushion (pillow), so that you can take accurate measurements.
- AN IRON. To press all the seams and make sure your cushion cover looks nice and crisp.

METHOD

WASH AND IRON.

Before starting, wash and iron your fabric. This will make sure that when you wash the cushion (pillow) cover in the future, no shrinkage occurs.

CREATE YOUR PATTERN.

Measure the height and width of your cushion (pillow). On a piece of newspaper or wrapping paper, measure out a square that is 5cm (2in) bigger than your cushion (for example, if your cushion is 30cm/12in square, your paper square will be 35 x 35cm/14 x 14in). Cut this square out. This is **pattern piece 1** and will form the front of your cushion cover.

Next, cut a paper rectangle that is half the height of the square you just cut, but keep the same width (so, for our example, this would be 17.5cm x 35cm / 7 x 14in). This is **pattern piece 2**.

Finally, cut another paper rectangle that is two-thirds of the height of the square, but keep the same width (so 23.5 x 35cm/9¼ x 14in). This is **pattern piece 3**.

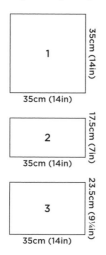

Pieces 2 and 3 will form the back of the 'envelope'.

PIN AND CUT.

Once you have all your pattern pieces, pin them to your fabric and cut out one of each piece. If you are using a patterned fabric, make sure you are pinning the pattern pieces from top to bottom (not left to right), so that the finished cushion (pillow) cover won't have a sideways pattern.

SEW.

Take pattern piece 2 and place it right side down on the table (see page 113 for 'right side'). Again, if you are using a patterned fabric, make sure the top of the design is at the top of the table. Fold the bottom raw edge of your pattern piece up 0.5cm (¼in) and press with an iron. Then fold the same edge another 0.5cm (¼in), so that the raw edge is hidden. Press with an iron and pin down. Then stitch along the line where the pins are, so that you are securing this outer hem.

Now take pattern piece 3 and repeat the process above to the top raw edge, rather than the bottom one. Pieces 2 and 3 should now have one long edge each that is hemmed.

CONNECT FRONT AND BACK.

Take piece 1 and place it wrong side down on the table (so the 'outside' of the fabric will be facing you). Now take piece 2 and place it right side down on top of piece 1, aligning the top and side edges. Finally, take piece 3 and place this on top of pieces 1 and 2, right side down, aligning the bottom and side edges. Pin all the way round.

Sew along all four sides,

taking a seam allowance of 1.5cm (⅝in). Go around twice to make sure it's all securely connected.

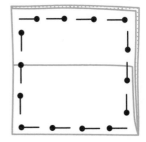

CLIP.

When you have finished sewing, clip the four corners diagonally (without cutting any stitching). This will make sure that the points are nice and sharp when you turn the cushion (pillow) cover out.

TURN OUTSIDE IN.

Turn the cover right way out and use a chopstick, pencil or your finger to push out the corners. Press all the seams so that they are nice and crisp.

FILL.

When you are happy with your corners, insert the cushion pad (pillow form) and you are done.

KEEPING GOING

Once you have mastered some basic sewing skills, you can move on to pattern-cutting, making and fitting clothes. One of the reasons a lot of people sew is because they want to wear better fitting clothes that reflect their personal style. Wearing garments that you love and make you feel great is an incredible feeling and provides a real boost to your confidence.

There is a multitude of free online resources that will guide you through your sewing education.

Have a search around for the one that suits you best, but the following provide a good starting point:

MADE TO SEW. YouTube channel Made to Sew (www.youtube.com/madetosew) is fantastic. It will take you right the way from learning the essentials, such as knowing which thread to pick and threading your machine, to the trickiest technical details. And it's all free!

TILLY AND THE BUTTONS (www.tillyandthebuttons.com) and SEW OVER IT (www.sewoverit.co.uk) are two great sites that provide tutorials, sew-a-longs, and downloadable pdf patterns, as well as access to a fun and sociable online community of sewers.

REMEMBER.

If you make a mistake, you can always unpick the thread! Sewing can be frustrating but keep going – the final result is always worth the effort.

KNIT (OR CROCHET)

Knitting, though complicated to get your head round at first, is one of the most satisfying things you can occupy your hands with as it is mostly repetitive, and so over time your brain will learn the technique automatically.

This means that it can be done almost without thinking about it, and so is perfect to do alongside other things like chatting or watching TV, making moments of downtime productive and leaving you with something to show for your time.

The tactility of knitting is also surprisingly effective. If your working week is made up of touchscreens and keyboards, spending some time with a pair of wooden knitting needles and some yarn between your fingers is a fantastic way to reconnect with the material world. The physical measurement of

your labour, as you witness your creation growing row-by-row, is second to none – especially when we are used to measuring our productivity by the volume of emails sent in a day, or the number of new spreadsheets created.

And last, but by no means least, knitting is a fantastic source of mental calm and clarity, bringing you to a state of focused attention and mindfulness and allowing you to observe your thoughts as you create.

LEARN TO KNIT

If you're able to learn from a friend or relative who is already well ahead on their knitting journey, having someone there to show you the movements will often make things easier. Don't forget, this could also be done via a video call if you're not living near each other! If this isn't an option, the next best way to develop your skills is to watch some online tutorials. WOOL AND THE GANG (www.woolandthegang. com) or LOVECRAFTS (www.lovecrafts.com) are fantastic resources full of free tutorials, patterns and all the basic essentials you need to get started. If learning by written instruction is more your thing, *Learn to Knit, Love to Knit* by Anna Wilkinson is a great place to start.

If you've never knitted before, a good project to start with is a chunky scarf. For this, you will need:

- Large knitting needles (10mm/US size 15 needles are perfect). Go for wooden needles if possible, as the wool will slip less than on metal ones.

- A good, chunky yarn.

- A beginner's tutorial to knitting a scarf. Again, Wool and the Gang have a really great one.

Unlike weaving, which interlaces two separate threads perpendicular to each other, knitting creates a meandering path with a single yarn. The result is an elastic and stretchy fabric – perfect for sweaters, hats, gloves, socks... and all sorts of comfortable, expandable and cosy clothing. Once you've got to know the basics, challenge yourself with some more complicated patterns.

CROCHET

If socks and sweaters aren't your thing, and you're looking to decorate your home more than yourself, crochet is a great alternative. Though knitting and crochet are both methods of looping yarn together, knitting uses two needles – moving a set of loops from one needle to another – while crochet uses a single hook, connecting the loops together directly on the piece of crochet. The result is a slightly stiffer fabric, ideal for blankets and table runners, although you can start with something as simple as a headband or a cup-cosy for your coffee cup.

LEARN TO CROCHET

JAYDA IN STITCHES (www.jaydainstitches.com) or THE SPRUCE CRAFTS (www.thesprucecrafts. com) are just two free online resources that will provide you with all the basic information, plus video tutorials, to take your skill level from novice to expert.

A good project to get started with is a simple square as these form the basis of lots of things, from coasters to blankets to garments. You will need:

- A crochet hook – anything between 5.5–7mm (US sizes I-9–K-10½) is good for beginners.
- Scissors
- A yarn needle
- Some yarn – acrylic yarn is good to start with because it is inexpensive and so will allow you to experiment. Different yarn weights work with different hook sizes, so ask for help when choosing your yarn (or if ordering online, it should always say on the yarn label what size hook to use with that specific yarn).

REMEMBER.

If you make a mistake, you can always unravel it and start again. Your first few goes might include quite a lot of unravelling, but don't give up. Eventually, it will click and, once it does, it will become second nature.

MACRAMÉ

Macramé is a retro craft that has never completely fallen out of style. As a process, it's a very easy, accessible and satisfying way to create things for your home, and gifts for your friends.

A fun project to start with is a macramé hanging plant holder. Whether it's part of a boho chic living room or for adding some green to your bathroom by creating a holder for your favourite succulent, it's a perfect way to breathe some new life into an interior.

Once you've mastered this basic design, browse the internet to find a wealth of more complex and impressive patterns to weave into your home.

THINGS YOU NEED:

- Wool, rope or macramé cording (available at craft stores)
- Scissors
- Metal or wooden ring
- Some sort of container for your plant: terracotta pots, glass bowls or tin cans all work well. If using a ceramic pot, think about whether you'd like to decorate it by painting it first.
- Ruler or tape measure

METHOD

MEASURE.

Work out how long you want your hanging plant holder to be (i.e. how far down you want it to hang from the ceiling or a hook). Add about 30cm (12in) to this, just to be sure it won't end up too short, then cut eight equal lengths of string or cord to this measurement. Align all eight pieces at one end, and tie them together in a knot at that end. This will be the bottom of your holder, so if you want it to appear as a tassel, make sure you tie the knot a short way up.

While you have the measuring tape out, measure the height of the pot you wish to suspend in the macramé holder. Multiply this number by 0.4. The value you get is a rough estimate of how far apart your knots should be spaced (in either inches or centimetres) when you get to that step.

DIVIDE.

Next, divide the eight pieces of string into four groups of two and spread them out like a cross. Tie each set together about 2.5cm (1in) up from your first knot. It will look a little like a flower at this point.

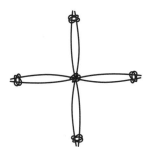

Next, pick up the left string from one set of strings and tie it to the right string from the set right next to it. (Use the measurement you found in the first step to establish roughly how far apart this row of knots should be from your first row of knots. In this example, the second row of knots should be 9cm (3½in) above the first row of knots.) Repeat this step for the remaining three sets of strings.

REPEAT.

Repeat the same process as described in the above step for the third row of knots. When it's spread out, you should notice a flower shape within a square shape.

POSITION.

After your knots are tied, place your pot so that the tassel is centred on the bottom of it. Bring up all four sets of string and adjust the pot as necessary, so that the strings are fairly evenly spaced around it and it hangs straight.

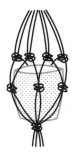

FINISH.

Gather all strings up above the pot and tie a ring onto all strings at the height that you would like to hang the pot from. Trim the excess string.

REMEMBER.

Plant holders make a really lovely gift (if you can include the plant as well, even better!).

PRINT

Although there are five main types of printmaking (relief, monotype, intaglio, silkscreen and lithography), relief printing is the best place to start, as it is the most accessible and least intimidating.

Relief printing is when the ink sits on the surface of a plate or block that has been carved. If you ever made a potato stamp as a child, you are already one relief print down! You can print in relief on a variety of surfaces, though the two most common are linoleum (lino) and woodcut. If you are a beginner, lino is best to start with: wood can be more challenging as you have to make sure you carve in the direction of the grain in order to get smooth lines, which takes time and experimentation. Lino is inexpensive and durable, and has a smooth surface without grain or direction.

A quick google of 'lino printmaking kit' will return several good results of 'starter packs' to get you going with the essential equipment. These should include a cutter or 'burin' with several different cutter-heads that you can swap in (based on the effect you'd like to achieve), a few sheets of lino, an ink roller, an ink tray, some printing ink and a hand guard for when you are cutting.

You will also need some paper. Lightweight paper is best for printing at home (without a press) as you won't need to apply too much pressure to get a good impression. Matt finishes are also good as the ink won't run or smudge. Don't go for anything too textured (for example, some handmade papers) as the fibres and flecks within the paper can make the surface quite rough and this causes problems when trying to get a consistent or solid impression of your linocut. If you're starting out, you could use something as basic as a matt, 120–150gsm printer paper – the lower cost will mean you have more opportunity for experimentation and getting it right! Once you feel more confident, move up to a slightly more expensive paper – a lot of printers recommend Japanese paper.

The joy of printing lies as much in the fact that you can make multiple copies of your design as it does in the actual design, so don't panic too much about producing an intricate or complex design on your first go – just enjoy the batch production of it! Start with a simple line drawing or a bold geometric pattern. As a beginner, your style will be fairly heavy and a bit wobbly, so embrace this: don't try and be too delicate. Once you've got your technique down, you can start producing some more intricate designs that could be used for greeting cards, wrapping paper, or limited edition prints for friends and family.

HOW TO MAKE A LINO PRINT

PREPARE THE DESIGN.

On a piece of paper the same size as your print, use a pencil to draw a simple black-and-white design. When ready, place the pencil drawing face down on to the lino. To transfer the drawing onto the lino block, rub the back of the paper with your fingers or, if that doesn't work, use a pencil or pen to shade in the area that covers your design. With this method, you don't need to worry about reversing the image, as it will happen naturally when you transfer it from the paper to the block. If you are drawing directly onto the lino, and not using the paper method, you will need to reverse the image first.

ink (the bits you cut away will be white or blank on the paper).

CUT.

Before you start cutting your design out, practise on a separate piece of lino. Your cutter will have come with a range of different heads, varying from shallow U-shaped cuts (good for cutting out big chunks) to more defined V-shaped cuts (good for detail). Get to know the feeling and effect of each head, and how to handle the cutter. Short cuts are easier than long ones; and you'll get a better result if you don't dig the cutter into the lino but try to keep it flat on the surface of the block. Always cut away from yourself and always use the hand guard!

INK.

Once you've finished cutting, roll out your ink on the ink tray. Roll the ink in different directions to get an even amount on the roller. When you're ready, apply the ink to the raised surface of your lino cut.

When you feel you've had a few good practice rounds, start cutting out your design. Remember that you are cutting away the areas that will NOT take up the

APPLY THE PAPER.

Place your chosen piece of paper on top of the inked image and apply some pressure to transfer the ink onto the paper. Some printing kits will come with a baren (a disc-shaped hand-press that you can use to distribute the pressure evenly). If you don't have one of these, your fingertips or your palms.

REVEAL.

Once you're sure you've applied even amounts of pressure around the paper and the print, slowly peel the paper off the lino block to reveal the printed image. Don't be discouraged if the first print is a bit blotchy. Sometimes it takes a few goes to get the right amount of ink and pressure.

REVIEW AND REPEAT.

Now that you have your first print, check if there are any areas that need more cutting (perhaps you didn't cut deep enough or you missed an area) and, once you're satisfied, get batch producing!

REMEMBER.

Embrace the chunkiness! The more it looks like a handmade print, the better – so don't worry about little mistakes and blotches, they will make your prints more unique.

GARDEN

Gardening is a bit like alchemy, in that by bringing bulbs and seeds together with earth, water and light, we can give life to the most mind-bogglingly beautiful and complex plants.

It's a real lesson in how the labours of our hands can reap rewards for all our senses – smell, sight, touch, and sometimes even taste. It also has incredible benefits for the mind: the cycle of sow and reap provides a good metaphor for life, and helps us understand the value of nurture, time and patience; as well as not to be afraid of decay, as there will always be renewal.

Witnessing plants grow is also a brilliant reminder of the year's cycle and makes you notice changes in the weather and climate more keenly. Sitting at a desk all day, as most of us

do, with only a glimpse through a window of the outside world, time can begin to feel uniform and monotonous. Even if you only have space for a few pot plants on a windowsill, gardening still provides a sense of greater connection to the natural world and the seasons.

Finally, the tactility of gardening makes it an almost primitive delight. There's something therapeutic in digging our hands into the soil. Getting our hands dirty in the garden supposedly also has its health benefits: from boosting our immune systems through bringing us into contact with more bacteria, to allowing us to absorb essential nutrients found in the soil through our skin, for example phosphorus, potassium, calcium and magnesium. On top of this, the added dose of Vitamin D – if you are gardening outside – boosts immunity, mood and sleep quality.

GET POTTING

Whether you live in an apartment block or a house with a garden, the following plants are easy to pot and will grow well both inside and outside (during warmer months):

FLOWERS.

While most spring flowers need to be chilled at temperatures of 1–7°C (35–45°F) for up to 15 weeks – making them hard to grow indoors as it's unlikely you'll have a room constantly at this temperature – bulbs that are native to warm climates don't require a cooling period to trigger blooms. Amaryllis and Paperwhite Narcissus both belong in this category.

AMARYLLIS. Amaryllis bulbs are best planted in a pot filled with soil, with about a third of the bulb above the soil line. Place in bright, indirect light and water sparingly until growth begins in earnest. Amaryllis are available in many interesting colours and forms: bright reds, white, pink, peach, and even green!

PAPERWHITE NARCISSUS. Paperwhite bulbs can either be planted or just placed in a shallow bowl, using pebbles to hold the bulbs in place. Add water, and they'll usually bloom just four weeks after 'planting'. To help keep stems short and sturdy, start them out with indirect light and temperatures of about 10°C (50°F) for the first two weeks; then warmer, brighter conditions after that. If you're growing your bulbs in a bowl with pebbles or marbles, the water should cover no more than the bottom quarter to third of the bulb.

Paperwhites offer delicate beauty and an intense fragrance. Buy a few dozen bulbs and store them in a cool, dry place. Start some every few weeks in late winter for blooms right through spring.

HERBS.

Most herbs can be cultivated inside, easily sown from seed or bought from nurseries or garden centres. Good herbs to grow for use in cooking include:

- Basil
- Chives
- Lemon balm
- Marjoram
- Mint (chocolate mint, peppermint, spearmint, or sweet mint)
- Oregano (Greek oregano, Italian oregano, or hot and spicy oregano)
- Parsley (flat Italian parsley or curled parsley)
- Rosemary
- Sage
- Thyme (German thyme or lemon thyme)

SUNLIGHT. To grow well indoors, herbs need as much natural light as possible. Place them in a sunny spot near a window that faces south and receives at least 6 hours of sun daily. Some herbs that require less light (like mint, parsley and thyme) can also grow well in west-facing windows. Be sure to keep an eye out for signs that your herbs are not getting enough light. These include poor growth, stems that grow unusually long between leaf sets, leaves that are smaller than usual, and stems or leaves that are abnormally pale or begin to turn yellow. If you can't get enough natural light to your plants, you can use a grow light, which mimics sunlight and should get your shoots sprouting.

TEMPERATURE. Indoor herbs prefer the same

temperatures that most people do, so if you're comfortable, they probably are. At night, temperatures near a window may drop, but most herbs like that, too, except for basil, which needs a pretty constant temperature of around 20°C (70°F) day and night. As a precaution, though, keep foliage from touching glass to protect the leaves from getting nipped by cold.

AIR. Dry air, whether from air conditioning or heating, is hard on most herbs, so you may want to consider increasing the surrounding humidity. Remember that the air next to a window will be cooler in winter (or hotter in summer) than your average indoor temperature, so adjust your plants accordingly.

POTS. The best way to ruin most herbs is to let them sit in water, which rots the roots. Clay pots are good for drainage, but they can dry out quickly. If you live in a dry climate or are growing herbs indoors during winter, when central heating causes homes to become especially dry, try a glazed or plastic container. Whatever pot you use, make sure it has a hole in the bottom, so that the water can drain. Place a saucer, liner or drain pan under the pot to catch water and protect your surfaces. A clay saucer lets moisture pass through, so opt for plastic, rubber, or metal instead.

REMEMBER.
Even though it might look like nothing is happening above the surface, everything is happening in the soil. Be patient and one day, when you've almost given up hope, your plant will suddenly burst into action.

WORK WITH CLAY

Clay is ubiquitous. Both malleable and solid, as a substance it has been sourced from the earth and manipulated in numerous ways and used for a variety of purposes for thousands of years.

Clay is fascinating in that it will lend itself to any level of skill. From clay figures and beads, to cooking pots and storage jars, to ovens, chimneys and bricks: the development of human history has gone hand in hand with our ability to work clay to our needs.

In addition to its physical qualities, certain clays are also good for us. Calcium bentonite clay is an absorbent kind of clay that typically forms after volcanic ash ages. This clay has a unique composition and can absorb 'negatively charged' toxins. People have been using calcium bentonite clay for centuries as a way to detoxify the body, improve digestion and skin tone, and more. Getting your hands stuck in to a lump of clay can therefore benefit you in more ways than one.

PINCH POTS

The potter's wheel did not appear in history until 4,000 years ago. Prior to that, pinch and coil construction methods prevailed as the main techniques humans used to form clay. Even today, pinching remains a valuable, creative and satisfying way to work with clay and can be used to form many types of pieces.

Pinch pots are easily accessible to nearly everyone, including young children, and are one of the most direct ways of interacting with clay. You push, and the clay responds. You pinch, and again the clay responds. You can learn a huge amount simply through the experience of directly modifying the clay's form. Pinching also teaches tactile sensitivity: through this process, you learn to rely on your fingers to tell you information about the clay.

WHAT YOU NEED.

If you decide to enrol on a beginners' pottery course, you will be provided with all the tools and materials that you need to get going. This will most likely include a stoneware clay, which will need firing in a kiln to convert it from a weak clay into a strong, durable, crystalline-like form.

For those of you undertaking this at home, without the help of a kiln, an air-dry clay will do perfectly for ornamental pinch pots (but please don't eat or drink from them, as air-dry clay is not foodsafe). This can be ordered online or found at your local art store, or if you prefer a more consolidated starter pack, SCULPD (www.sculpd.co.uk), ETSY (www.etsy.com) or SCULPEY (www.sculpey.com) produce fantastic kits, with everything you need for getting going at home, including the clay.

In addition, you'll need:

- An apron
- A small bowl for holding water as you work
- A large, soft brush – a large paintbrush will do
- A trimming tool – these are usually wooden, but a blunt knife will work just as well
- A cutting wire – any thick wire from the toolbox will work

YOUR SET-UP.

Regardless of whether you are in a studio or in your kitchen, make sure you have the following set-up to ensure minimal mess:

- Floors that are easy to clean and impervious to water, such as concrete or linoleum

- Access to water (but no clay should go down any drains!)

- A sturdy table, such as a kitchen table

- A surface to work on, that clay won't stick to (best to use an oilcloth tablecloth, with a piece of canvas beneath your clay so that you can rotate it without having to lift it every time)

- A shelf for drying pots, out of the reach of little hands

METHOD

ROLL.

Roll a small ball of clay, about the size of a clementine orange, between your hands.

Holding the ball in one hand, slowly push the thumb of the other hand into the centre of the clay.

PINCH.

Gently pinch the clay between your thumb on the inside, and your fingers on the outside while slowly turning the ball of clay in your hand.

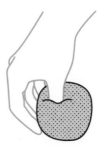

Work in a spiral from bottom to top. If you want to make your pot more bowl-like, you can pinch the top open more broadly and thinly, although make sure your clay isn't too wet when doing this or it will struggle to hold its shape.

TAP.

Gently tap the pot on the table to make a flat base.

REPAIR.

Repair deep cracks immediately, using a tiny amount of water or slip (clay mixed with water to create a gravy-like texture). If necessary, use your brush to smooth over cracks.

FINISH.

When you're finished, use a blunt knife to trim the rim of your pot or bowl.
   Leave to dry.

SAND.

If using air-dry clay, once the clay has dried, sand it down and think about whether or not you'd like to paint it. A white base is a good place to start, and allows you to add colourful decorations on top.

REMEMBER.

Clay is one of the oldest materials that humans have worked with – it's not something special reserved only for top ceramicists and artists. Don't be intimidated and, as ever, if it doesn't work out the first time, just keep practising.

BAKE

There is nothing like the taste, smell and texture of freshly baked bread.

Both the sensory experience and the reward of creating your own basic nourishment make baking bread an all-round comforter. A huge amount of people turned to baking bread at the start of the Covid-19 lockdown. If still feel that bread is too complicated to make from scratch, even just reading through this incredibly easy recipe will make you feel more confident.

REALLY EASY BREAD RECIPE

PREPARATION TIME:
20 minutes
RISING TIME:
1–2 hours (you can leave it while it rises)
COOKING TIME:
30–35 minutes

INGREDIENTS.

- 500g (3½ cups) strong bread flour
- 7g (¼oz) sachet fast-action dried yeast
- 1 tsp salt
- 300ml (1¼ cups) hand-hot water
- 2 tbsp sunflower oil
- 1 tbsp honey

METHOD.

Tip the flour into a bowl and mix in the yeast with the salt. Stir in the water, oil and honey. Now bring together to make a soft dough using your hands, or use a wooden spoon.

Lightly flour a surface. Tip the dough onto the surface and knead for 10 minutes. You might want to watch an online tutorial on 'How to knead' if you've never done this before. Essentially, you are using the heels of your hands to push the dough down and outwards from the centre; then folding in half, turning 45 degrees and repeating for the full 10 minutes. It is worth putting in the time to do this as it will pay off later with lovely airy bread.

Don't keep adding flour – a wet dough is better than a dry one, which will bake to a tough texture – so if you don't like the dough sticking to your hands, lightly oil them.

Turn the dough into an oiled 1kg (2lb) bread tin (pan) and cover with oiled clingfilm (plastic wrap) – this will stop the bread from drying out. Put in a warm place until the bread fills the tin. This should take 1–2 hours.

Preheat the oven to 200°C/180°C fan/400°F/gas 6. Uncover and bake your bread in the preheated oven for 30–35 minutes until golden. Tip out of

the tin and tap the base of the loaf. It should sound hollow when fully baked. If not, put the loaf back in the oven out of the tin and test again after 10 minutes. Leave to cool before slicing.

KEEP LEARNING

Once you've mastered a basic loaf of bread, you can branch out to more diverse and elaborate recipes. There are hundreds of free recipes online for different types of bread and pastries, as well as online tutorials on sites like www.breadahead. com or www.breadtopia. com, where you can learn a whole host of new techniques.

REMEMBER.

Don't tell yourself that this will take you 3 hours to make: you don't have to hang around while the dough is rising. Let it do its thing while you go out to meet a friend, so that you can come home and pop it straight in the oven.

EXERCISE

The benefits of exercise are countless and self-evident, and need little introduction. Exercise makes us buzz, it makes us burn and it makes our bodies function at their optimum.

However, if you're used to working out in a gym, it's likely that your hand muscles aren't getting much of a look-in, beyond holding onto handlebars. No doubt there have been many times when you have returned from a gym session and remarked on how your abs, your thighs or your glutes are burning – but have you ever noticed your hands feeling this way? Your hands enjoy just as much exercise: there are over 30 muscles which move the fingers and thumb, and they all love a bit of attention.

The following types of exercise rely on your hands just as much as the rest of your body.

ROCK-CLIMBING

How better to discover the power of your strength than to be able to support your own body weight while scaling a wall?

When starting out rock-climbing, *never* go at it alone. If the great outdoors is your nearest gym, join a climbing club and make the group aware that you are a novice. If you're in a city, join a gym with a climbing wall and make sure you get as much training and support as you need. You should be introduced to the following types of climbing:

GYM CLIMBING

Gyms attempt to replicate outdoor climbing experiences through the use of artificial walls, handholds, and footholds. At each gym, different 'routes' up the wall are set at varying levels of difficulty. Routes are typically colour-coded by holds, and their difficulty is marked at the start with a plastic card designating its name and grade. The higher the number, the more difficult the route.

BOULDERING

The biggest distinction between bouldering and other types of climbing is that in bouldering there is no use of a rope or harness. Instead of relying on ropes for protection, bouldering usually relies on crash pads (thick padded mats) to protect climbers when they fall. Additionally, routes (called 'problems' in bouldering) are not typically more than 6m

(2oft) tall. Because minimal equipment is needed (usually just climbing shoes and chalk for your hands) and little initial training is necessary, bouldering has a low barrier of entry. As such, it's often the starting point for many new climbers.

TOP-ROPING

If you're climbing indoors but not bouldering, chances are you're top-roping. These climbs are protected by a rope anchored from above and belayed (the act of applying tension to the rope to minimize the distance in a fall) from the ground. Top-roping is usually considered less physically demanding than other types of climbing due to the belayer's ability to prevent the climber from taking large falls. As such, it's probably the most popular type of indoor roped-climbing.

SPORT (LEAD) CLIMBING

Sport lead climbing relies on fixed bolts for protection along a pre-defined route. The lead climber ascends the route with the rope tied to his or her harness and clips into each bolt or quickdraw to protect against a fall. In indoor climbing gyms, quickdraws are pre-placed on the bolts so that a lead climber only has to clip the rope in as he or she ascends the route.

TAKING IT OUTDOORS

While indoor facilities provide a safe and convenient environment in which to practise, climbing can enjoyed more fully in the great outdoors — where the weather, rocks and scenery are constantly changing. Indoor and outdoor climbing have many of the same gear requirements, and both types of climbing utilize many of the same skills.

If you're comfortable climbing indoors, there's no reason why you shouldn't try it outside, although, due to the ever-changing natural environment, make sure you join a climbing group when transitioning from indoor to outdoor, so that you have maximum knowledge, protection and support.

PADDLE-BOARDING

Paddle boarding is a unique activity for the entire body, led by your hands, wrists, arms and shoulders. It also requires a lot of core and leg strength to keep yourself balanced on the board. In short, it is a whole-body workout.

One of the best things about paddle-boarding is that it is a low-impact workout, meaning it can't do serious damage to your ligaments or tendons. This makes it a great form of exercise for anyone that experiences knee or hip pain, or shin splints, as it can help increase strength or help you recover from injuries, without doing any harm to your body. That being said, you must be a good swimmer when undertaking paddle-boarding, as it takes a lot of practice to hone your balance on the board, and it's likely you'll fall into the water multiple times before you get the hang of it.

The best way to start paddle-boarding is to take part in a class. This way, you don't need to invest in any expensive equipment and can get to know whether or not this is the sport for you. If you live in a city, paddle-boarding classes often take place in indoor pools or on local rivers and ponds. Needless to say, as an activity, paddle-boarding is definitely more fun when surrounded by warm water.

ALTERNATIVES TO PADDLE-BOARDING:
Canoeing if you prefer not to exercise your legs; or rowing if you still want to exercise legs but want to decrease the risk of falling in the water!

BOXING

Although traditionally a combat sport, boxing doesn't have to mean sparring against an opponent (unless you want it to). Many gyms offer 'Box-Fit' classes: a combination of boxing against a bag and circuit training. There's some strange connection between boxing and the brain. While discovering the strength of your fists and arms, you somehow gain a sense of your mental robustness at the same time. It teaches you that you are strong and in control, not to mention gives you a great whole-body workout.

Other hand-orientated sports to consider: Tennis, squash, ping-pong, fencing, archery, darts. Remember: your hands are lean, mean muscle machines.

ACKNOWLEDGMENTS

I am hugely indebted to the many thinkers mentioned in this book who have expanded my understanding of the world, bringing fascination, clarity and reassurance at times when I've most needed it.

This book also wouldn't exist without the great enthusiasm, encouragement and patience of my agent Louise Lamont, editor Céline Hughes, and the fantastic team at Quadrille!

Finally, I can never go without acknowledging the endless sparks of joy that are my family and friends – who make optimizing every second of my life far too easy.

PUBLISHING DIRECTOR:
SARAH LAVELLE

SENIOR COMMISSIONING EDITOR: CÉLINE HUGHES

SENIOR DESIGNER:
EMILY LAPWORTH

ILLUSTRATIONS:
SARAH FISHER

HEAD OF PRODUCTION:
STEPHEN LANG

PRODUCTION CONTROLLER:
SINEAD HERING

Published in 2021 by Quadrille, an imprint of Hardie Grant Publishing

Quadrille
52–54 Southwark Street
London SE1 1UN
quadrille.com

Cataloguing in Publication Data: a catalogue record for this book is available from the British Library

Text © Laura Archer 2021
Illustrations © Sarah Fisher 2021
Design and layouts © Quadrille 2021

ISBN 978 1 78713 550 5

Printed in China